G000149620

Getting Started with Your Mac and Mac OS X Tiger

Scott Kelby

PEACHPIT LEARNING SERIES

GETTING STARTED WITH YOUR MAC AND MAC OS X TIGER: PEACHPIT LEARNING SERIES

Scott Kelby
Copyright © 2005 by Scott Kelby

Published by Peachpit Press. For information on Peachpit Press books, contact:

Peachpit Press
1249 Eighth Street
Berkeley, CA 94710
510-524-2178 voice
510-524-2111 fax
www.peachpit.com

To report errors, please send a note to errata@peachpit.com
Peachpit Press is a division of Pearson Education

Composed in Myriad Pro, Minion Pro, and Helvetica by KW Media Group

ISBN 0-321-33052-8
9 8 7 6 5 4 3 2
Printed and bound in the United States of America

www.scottkelbybooks.com

The Getting Started with Your Mac and Mac OS X Tiger Team

CREATIVE DIRECTOR
Felix Nelson

TECHNICAL EDITOR
Polly Reincheld

COPY EDITOR
Veronica Martin

PRODUCTION EDITOR
Kim Gabriel

PRODUCTION MANAGER
Dave Damstra

COVER DESIGNED BY
Felix Nelson

PHOTOS BY
Scott Kelby

For my good friend Terry White, also known as the central clearinghouse of all Macintosh knowledge.

ACKNOWLEDGMENTS

Although only one name appears on the spine of this book, it takes a large, dedicated team of people to put a book like this together. Not only did I have the good fortune of working with such a great group of people, I now get the great pleasure of thanking them and acknowledging their hard work and dedication.

First, I want to thank my amazing wife Kalebra. She's just about the coolest person on this planet, and I am—without a doubt—the luckiest guy in the world to have her for my wife. I also want to thank our 8-year-old son Jordan for being, as I've said many times before, the greatest little boy in the whole wide world.

My heartfelt thanks to everybody on my creative team at KW Media Group who every day redefine what teamwork and dedication are all about. Special thanks to my Creative Director Felix Nelson who—as always—rocked the house, and to Dave Damstra for giving the book such a tight, clean look.

A big thanks to my tech editor Polly Reincheld for her invaluable help, advice, and for keeping everything organized and rolling along. Also thanks to my buddy Dave Moser, who convinced me years ago that I should be writing Mac books, and thanks to Jean A. Kendra for her support and enthusiasm for my book projects.

Thanks to Kathy "Miss Kathy" Siler, my wonderful assistant and hopelessly dedicated Redskins fan, who will once again feel the wrath of my Tampa Bay Bucs this year, unless of course we stink again.

Many thanks to my friends at Peachpit, especially my publisher Nancy Ruenzel. They really "get it," and their philosophy and vision make writing books an awful lot of fun, which is very rare in this industry. Also my thanks to Scott Cowlin and Rachel Tiley for tirelessly finding an audience for my books.

I want to thank all my "Mac Buddies" who've taught me so much over the years, including Bill Carroll, Jim Goodman, Dick Theriault, Don Wiggins, Dave Gales, Jim Workman, Jon Gales, Jim Nordquist, Rod Harlan, and Terry White.

Most importantly, I want to thank God, and His son Jesus Christ, for leading me to the woman of my dreams, for blessing us with such a special little boy, for allowing me to make a living doing something I truly love, for always being there when I need Him, for blessing me with a wonderful, fulfilling, and happy life, and such a warm, loving family to share it with.

Scott is Editor-in-Chief and co-founder of *Photoshop User* magazine, Editor-in-Chief of *Nikon Digital Pro* magazine, Editor-in-Chief of *Layers* magazine (the how-to magazine for everything Adobe), and is Executive Editor of the *Photoshop Elements Techniques* newsletter.

He is President of the National Association of Photoshop Professionals (NAPP), the trade association for Adobe® Photoshop® users, and he's President of the software training and publishing firm, KW Media Group, Inc.

Scott is an award-winning author of more than 26 books on Photoshop, digital imaging, and technology. In 2004, he was the world's #1 best-selling author of all computer and technology books. His other titles include *Mac OS X Killer Tips, Macintosh: The Naked Truth, Photoshop Down & Dirty Tricks*. Scott is also co-author of *Photoshop Killer Tips* and creator and Series Editor for the entire *Killer Tips* series from New Riders.

Scott's latest books include *The iPod Book* and *The Book for Guys Who Don't Want Kids (How to Get Past the Fear of Fatherhood)*. In 2004 Scott was awarded the publishing industry's prestigious Benjamin Franklin Award for his book *The Photoshop CS Book for Digital Photographers*.

Scott is Training Director for the Adobe Photoshop Seminar Tour, Conference Technical Chair for the Photoshop World Conference & Expo, and Training Director for the Mac Design Conference and Digital Photography Expo.

For more background info on Scott, visit www.scottkelby.com.

TABLE OF CONTENTS

www.scottkelbybooks.com

Really?

Absolutely. It's a time-honored tradition that all computer books make you (the reader) wait until everything has been explained fully, in great detail, before you're allowed to do anything.

In fact, many books make you start by reading chapters on the history of computing, followed by in-depth looks at how computers work, and what a "bit" and a "byte" are, and blah, blah, blah—all before they let you do anything. I call these "tell-me-all-about-it" books.

But this book breaks that mold. It's a "show-me-how-to-do-it" book, so instead of explaining all that junk that most people don't really care about, I show you, right from the beginning, step-by-step how to do the things you bought your Mac for in the first place.

The whole book is tutorial-based, so you'll be learning to do the things you really want to do, right off the bat: stuff like getting on the Internet, sending email, working with photos from your digital camera, downloading and importing music. You know, the fun stuff.

So where should you start?

If you've never used a computer before (and therefore, you probably don't know how to use a mouse), turn to Lesson 0, where I take just a few moments to taunt and ridicule you (kidding). Lesson 0 isn't really a lesson—it's just four pages—but if you don't know how to use a mouse or double-click, they may be the most important four pages in the book.

So, if you know how to use a mouse, you can jump straight to Lesson 1. However, it will help you along your path to Macintosh enlightenment if you go through the book in order: Lesson 1, Lesson 2, Lesson 6 (just seeing if you were paying attention), etc. That's because later lessons build on what you've learned in previous lessons. Now, do you have to go in that order? Absolutely not, because I'm pretty careful about spelling everything out, so if you really want to download some songs, connect your iPod, and go, you can do just that by turning to the music lesson (Lesson 3) and following my step-by-step instructions.

So I get to start doing fun stuff now?

Yup. Now, Lesson 1 is about setting up your Address Book, which may not sound like that much fun at first, but when you compare it to a chapter on the history of personal computing, it's absolutely riveting. Actually, what makes it fun is how brilliantly Apple has designed even simple things like the Address Book, so I thought it would be a great place to start—so turn the page, and start using your Mac now!

0

Time

Goals

This lesson takes approximately 3 minutes to complete.

To learn how to navigate around on the screen, double-click to launch an application, and quit an application using the mouse.

Four Things You Might Need to Know First

Now, I'm guessing that if you bought this book, you've already mastered the basics of using a mouse, and you know how to launch (and quit) the software applications on your Mac. But that's just a guess, and that's also why I used the word "might" in the lesson title. You *might* not know that stuff, and if that's the case, there are four key things that you're going to need to know before we can start the lessons in this book. They are: (1) How to move around the screen using a mouse; (2) how to double-click the mouse button; (3) how to launch an application; and (4) how to quit out of an application. Now, how hard is it to learn these four things? They're a breeze, and that's why I've only dedicated four pages in the book to learning them. Yes, these four things are critical things, but they're also very, very easy, so let's get right to it—turn the page and we'll go over all four. *Note:* If you already know how to use the mouse (double-click, etc.), you can skip the next few pages and catch up with me at Lesson 1.

*The cursor (arrow) is
moving toward an icon.*

*By clicking on the icon once using
the mouse, the icon is selected.*

Moving Around Your Mac Using a Mouse:
If you have a desktop Mac (like an iMac, a Power Mac G5, a Mac mini, or an eMac), you'll be using a mouse to move around the screen, to select different objects and menus, and to click on things you want to work with. Using a mouse is fairly simple—as you slide the mouse around on your desk, you'll see an arrow move around onscreen. If you see something you want to work with, just slide your mouse until the onscreen cursor (the arrow) is directly on top of that object, then press down lightly on your mouse and release. You'll hear a little "click" sound. That's "clicking," so in this book when I say something like "click on the icon" that means to move your mouse so the onscreen cursor is directly over the object, then lightly press and release your mouse so you hear the click sound. That's it.

Clicking just once will only select the folder.

Double-clicking rapidly using the mouse will open the folder.

How to Double-Click (and Why You'd Want to):
Double-clicking is what we do when we want to "start the action" (so to speak). For example, if you just click once on a folder, that folder is selected (it changes color so you know you've selected it), but nothing else happens. If you want to actually look inside the folder to view its contents, then you would need to double-click (which just means pressing down on the mouse twice in rapid succession, and by rapid I mean two clicks as fast as you can do them). It shouldn't be click…click (with a slight pause in between); it should be click-click!

How to Launch an Application:

In this book, we'll launch all our software applications (except one) by using the Dock that appears along the bottom of your screen (it's shown above). Each application is represented by a small image called an "icon." (*Note:* If you're not sure which icon represents the application you want to launch, let your arrow cursor hover over the icon and the name of the application will appear near your cursor.) To launch an application from the Dock, you just move your mouse so that the arrow cursor appears right over the application you want to launch, then click (press the mouse down and release) only once. In a few moments, the application will appear onscreen. To know which applications are open, look for a black triangle below each icon. If the icon has a black triangle beneath it, that application has been launched and is open for you to use.

How to Switch Between Applications:

You can switch between open applications anytime by moving your arrow cursor down to the Dock at the bottom of your screen, then moving it directly over the icon for the application you want to switch to and clicking once on it. You can also switch right from the keyboard itself by holding down the Command key (that's the key with the little Apple logo on it, found on both the immediate left and right of the Spacebar key), then tapping the Tab key on your keyboard. This brings up a large row of icons at the center of your screen for each open application (as shown above). To switch to another open application, keep holding down that Command key, then tap the Tab key. Each time you tap it, you select the next application's icon. When you've selected the one you want, just release the Command key.

1

Time

This lesson takes approximately 10 minutes to complete.

Goals

To get all names, addresses, phone numbers, and other contact info for your friends and family into your Mac's Address Book, so you can retrieve them anytime in just seconds.

How to Set Up Your Address Book

When you first considered getting a computer, I'm sure you probably thought about sending email, getting on the Internet, etc., and I'll bet you also thought about having all your software "work together," right? Right. Believe it or not, one of the cornerstones of making everything work together is to set up your Address Book (and by that I mean entering the name, address, phone number, and other contact info for your friends, relatives, companies you do business with, etc.). Luckily, there's an application that comes with Mac OS X Tiger called (surprisingly enough) Address Book. It does a wonderful job of managing all your addresses, and best of all, it shares this information with other software applications that you'll be using to simplify and organize your life (well, as far as your computing life goes, anyway). Now, don't worry if there seems to be a lot of steps to set up your Address Book—it's really simple and only takes a few minutes (unless, of course, you have hundreds of friends, in which case it'll take longer, but at least you'll have the consolation of knowing that you're obviously very popular).

STEP ONE:

Using your mouse, click once on the Address Book icon in the Dock at the bottom of your computer screen (its icon looks like a little brown book with a large white @ symbol on it).

STEP TWO:

The Address Book window will appear. The first time you launch Address Book, you'll see Apple Computer's contact info (just to give you an example of how a listing in your Address Book will look once you add your own entries). Besides Apple's contact info, you might also see a second name: "Admin User," or your own name. You can ignore that for now.

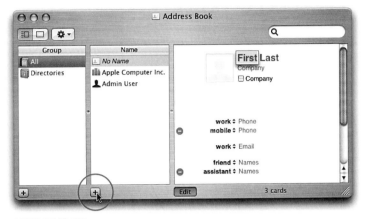

STEP THREE:

Now let's add someone to your Address Book. How 'bout me? Just in case you ever want to call. If you do, wait until after 10 p.m. EST when I'm sound asleep. To add me to your Address Book, start by clicking on the plus sign (+) button found just below the Name column near the left side.

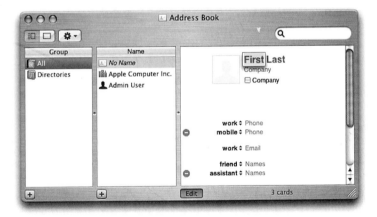

STEP FOUR:

This brings up a blank Name page, and if you look in the capture shown above, you'll see that the word "First" is highlighted for you. That's telling you to enter the person's first name (remember, for your first person you're entering my name, so using your keyboard type "Scott"). If you type the wrong letter, press the Delete key on your keyboard to erase your mistake.

STEP FIVE:

Once my first name is entered, press the Tab key on your keyboard to jump over to where you'll enter my last name (you can see the word "Last" highlighted in the capture shown above). Now type my last name, "Kelby." Again, if you make a mistake, press the Delete key to erase any wrong letters.

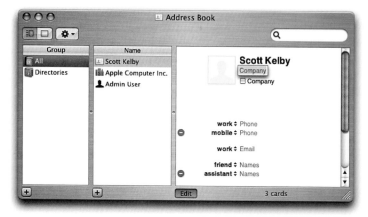

STEP SIX:

Once you've entered my first and last name, press the Tab key on your keyboard to move to the next entry—Company. Type "KW Media Group," then press Tab to jump to the Work Phone field.

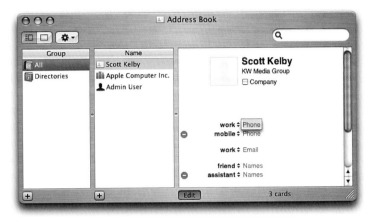

STEP SEVEN:

Now, let's type my work number: "813-433-5000." Once you've entered it, press the Tab key to jump down one field, in which you'll enter my cell phone number.

ENTERING NUMBERS

TIP ▶ When entering phone numbers, you don't have to add dashes between the numbers. Once you enter a number and press the Tab key to jump to the next field, Address Book automatically adds the dashes for you.

If you type it this way: Address Book formats it like this:
8134335000   813-433-5000

STEP EIGHT:

Apple set up the next line so you could enter the person's mobile (cellular) number, but what if you'd like to enter a person's home number first? (For our example, let's assume that you want my home number to appear directly below my work number.) To do that, just click once directly on the word "Mobile"—a menu listing alternate choices will appear.

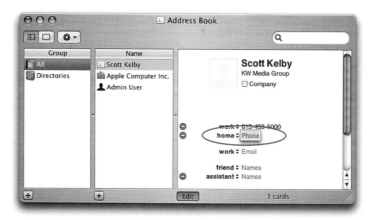

STEP NINE:

Using your mouse, move your arrow cursor up until "Home" is highlighted, then click the mouse button to select Home as the new name for this field. So, from now on, if you see a field and you want to change its name, you'll know what to do.

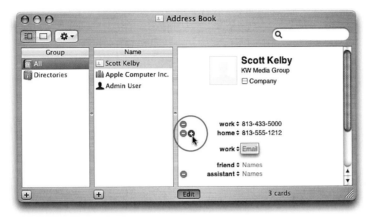

STEP TEN:
Once the field name has been changed to Home, enter my home number: "813-555-1212," and press the Tab key. Now the Work Email field is highlighted, and there's no mobile phone field (we replaced it with Home in the previous steps). So, to add an extra field (in this case, a field for my cell phone number), click on the green plus sign (+) button (shown circled above).

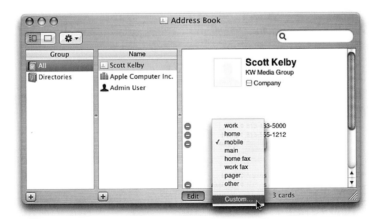

STEP ELEVEN:
When you click that button, a new Mobile Phone field is added directly below the Home Phone field. Personally, I never refer to my cell phone as my "mobile phone," so if you're like me, you'll want to change the name of this new field to Cell. Just click once on the word "Mobile" and choose Custom from the menu that appears.

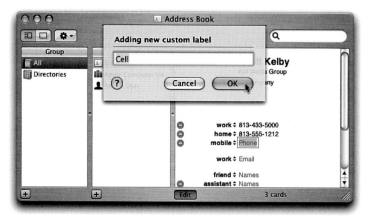

STEP TWELVE:

When you choose Custom, a little naming dialog pops down from the top of the Address Book window. Just type the new name (in this case, type the word "Cell") and click on the OK button. Now, this new field will be named Cell. Go ahead and type my cell number: "727-555-1214," and then press the Tab key to jump to the Work Email field.

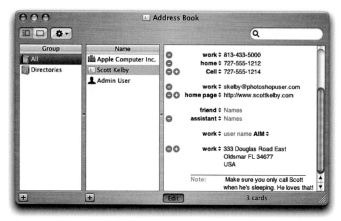

STEP THIRTEEN:

By now, I'm sure you see what comes next: You'll press the Tab key to get from line to line, typing in information. If you don't like the label for a field, you'll change it by clicking on the name and choosing a new one from the pop-up menu (or by choosing Custom from the pop-up menu and making your own). Fill in the rest of the card using the info I've entered above (you're doing this just to get the hang of it).

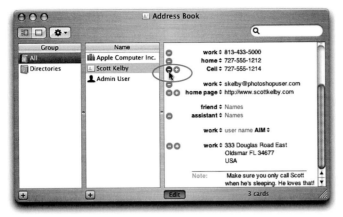

STEP FOURTEEN:

What if you decide you want to delete a field—then what? You do that by clicking on the little red minus button (–) to the left of the field. For example, let's say I asked you never to call me on my cell. You would delete my cell phone number by clicking on the red minus button to the left of the Cell Phone field. *Note:* You may not be able to delete some fields entirely because they're required by default. Fields with both a green plus and red minus sign can be deleted entirely by clicking on the red minus sign; otherwise, when you click the red minus sign, only the information in that field will be deleted.

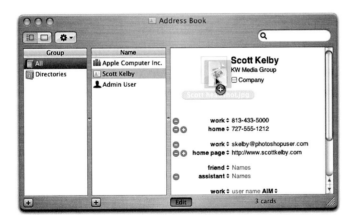

STEP FIFTEEN:

By the way, if you scroll to the top of the Name page (drag the blue gel-like bar on the right), you'll see a gray silhouette of a person's head in a box that appears to the immediate left of the person's name. This is where you can place a photo of that person. If you have a person's photo on your computer, find the photo on your hard disk, then click directly on it and drag-and-drop it right onto that little square. A little round green plus sign next to your pointer lets you know that the photo is being added.

STEP SIXTEEN:

When you drag-and-drop your photo on that square, a little window appears that shows you a preview of how that photo will look when it's shown in your Address Book. The slider underneath the preview makes the photo larger or smaller, so you can drag that slider to determine how the photo will fill the frame. Once the photo looks the way you want it to, click on the Set button.

STEP SEVENTEEN:

Now that you've added a photo, click the Edit button (shown circled above) to see how your final Address Book card will look. Now, you're going to repeat this same process to add all the people and companies that you want to appear in your Address Book. Once they're all added, you can put your Address Book to work.

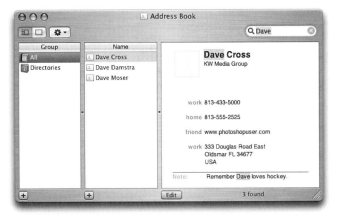

STEP EIGHTEEN:

Once you have a number of people added to your Address Book, finding them can be as easy as clicking on their name in the Name list in the center column. But if you've got more than 15 or 20 names, it's quicker to use the Search feature, found in the top-right corner of the Address Book window. Just type the first few letters of the person's name (or company name) in the Search field, and their name (along with anyone else with a similar name) will appear in the Name column.

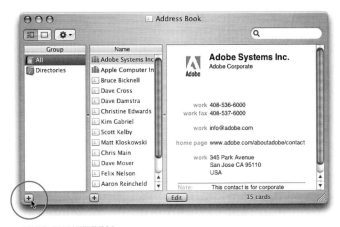

STEP NINETEEN:

Once you have a lot of contacts added to your Address Book, you can make finding people (and companies) easier by grouping things together (like one group with the phone numbers of all your favorite restaurants or one with all your co-workers). To do that, you start by clicking on the plus sign (+) button at the bottom of the first column (shown circled above).

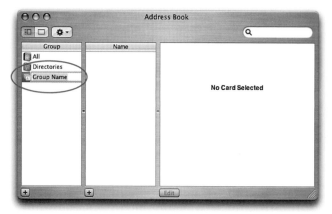

STEP TWENTY:

This adds a listing to the Group column (it's the first column from the left), and its current name, "Group Name," is already highlighted, meaning all you have to do is start typing your new name (in our example, I'm creating a group of my co-workers). After you've typed it in, press the Enter key on your keyboard to confirm your naming is complete.

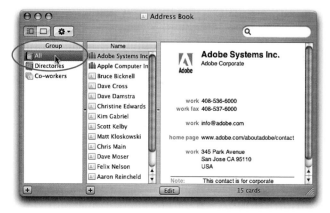

STEP TWENTY-ONE:

You'll want to add your co-workers' cards to that group. First, click on the All group (which appears at the very top of the Group column). This lists all of your address cards (you can see them listed in the Name column).

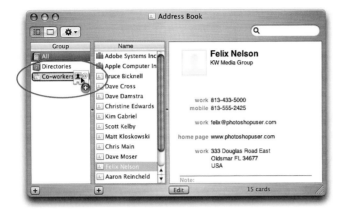

STEP TWENTY-TWO:

Now you just scroll through the Names column (by clicking-and-dragging the little blue pill-shaped button up and down) until you find the name of a co-worker. When you find a co-worker's name in the list, click-and-drag it to the Co-workers group that we created in the Group column, then release your mouse button.

STEP TWENTY-THREE:

Once you've added all your co-workers to your Co-workers group, click directly on that group in the Group column. Then you'll see why creating groups is so handy—now only your co-workers' cards are listed in the center Name column, making it easier to find the co-worker you're looking for. Now, in that Name column, just click on the co-worker's name to see that person's card (with phone number, address, picture, etc.).

2

Time

Goals

This lesson takes approximately 30 minutes to complete.

To organize and track your appointments for home and work; to create a custom calendar; and to use iCal's visual tools to keep everything instantly accessible and easy to use.

How to Set Up Your Calendar

You're going to set up your calendar (it's just like a regular calendar, where you can view holidays or note appointments, birthdays, work stuff, etc.). The idea behind iCal is to give you a simple way to differentiate all your various appointments with just a quick glance at your calendar. You do this by color coding your appointments. For example, you can have all your work appointments appear in one color (let's say green, for example), and all your home appointments appear in another color (let's say blue). That way, you can see exactly which appointments are which. But to take it a step further, you can turn off these sets of appointments, so you can see just your work appointments, or just your home appointments, or just holidays, or just…well, whatever you want because creating these individual color-coded calendars is simple.

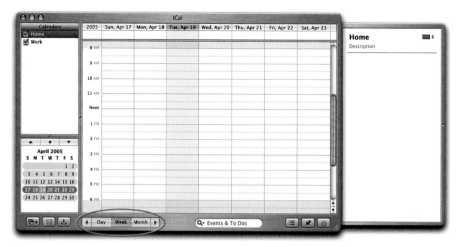

STEP ONE (Accessing iCal):

To open the iCal calendar program, click once on the iCal icon in the Dock at the bottom of your computer screen (looks like a desk calendar with a red bar across the top and the number 17 below). The first time you launch iCal, it opens in Week view, and you'll see today's date highlighted in light blue. By the way, you can see just today's appointments by clicking on the Day button in the bottom-left side of the iCal window, or to view the entire month, click the Month button.

STEP TWO (Preparing Your Home Calendar):

If you look in the top-left side of the iCal window, you'll see a Calendars panel, and listed in that panel are two views: Home (in blue) and Work (in green). They're different colors to help you visually keep track of which appointments are for your personal life (Home) and which are for work (you guessed it, Work). So, if you see an entry in green, you instantly know it's for work. But first, we're going to start by adding some appointments to your Home calendar, so in the Calendars list, click on Home (a blue highlight bar will appear over the word "Home" to let you know you're adding things to your Home calendar).

STEP THREE (Changing Months):

Because you're going to add a number of different appointments (called "Events") on different days of the month, it'll be easier to do this in the Month view. To switch to Month view, click on the Month button at the bottom of the iCal window, then click on the right-facing arrow button that appears just to the right of the Month button until August appears at the top of the window. (Why August? Because that's when the NFL preseason starts. What bearing does that have on this tutorial? None. I just like football.)

STEP FOUR (Adding a New Event):

Double-click in the white space in the center of the 7th day and a "New Event" (in blue) will appear. It's highlighted and ready for you to type a name for the event, so type "Scott's birthday," then press the Return key when you're done. (By the way, that's not my birthday, but it easily could've been if I were born a month later than I was.) Now, double-click in the white space on the 12th and add "Register Michael for school." (*Note:* Double-click on the white space to add an event; don't double-click on the date itself or iCal will switch to Day view.) On the 17th add "Meet repairman at house," and on the 22nd add "Dentist appt. at 2 p.m." This is pretty typical stuff that you might add to your calendar, especially if your son is named Michael, you've got a broken appliance, and you're coping with gingivitis.

STEP FIVE (Creating Events for a Work Calendar):

Now we'll add some business-related appointments in August, so in the Calendars list on the left side of iCal, click on the word "Work" (so your appointments will be added to the Work calendar). Double-click in the white space on the 5th and type "Meeting at 10 a.m.", then press the Return key to set that appointment. (You'll notice that this entry appears in green—the same color as your Work calendar.) On the 11th double-click and type "Second Quarter financials due," and on the 22nd add "Flight to Detroit at 7:30 p.m." (You already have an entry on the 22nd—on your Home calendar—so to add this, double-click in the white space below your Home appointment.)

CHANGING AND DELETING EVENTS

TIP If you've created an appointment, and need to change it (for example, if your 10:00 a.m. has been changed to 11:00 a.m.), you can just double-click directly on the event and it will highlight the text. Now you can type in your new information. If the meeting is cancelled altogether, just click on the appointment in your calendar, then press the Delete key.

STEP SIX (Easily View Specific Calendars):

Now that you've added events to both your Home and Work calendars, things can start to look a bit crowded, but that's where iCal shines. To see just your Work appointments instantly, go to your Calendars list (on the left side of the iCal window) and hide your Home appointments by turning off the checkbox to the left of Home. Now only your Work appointments are visible, so it's pretty easy to see—with just a glance—what's coming up for work. *Note:* To see your Home calendar again, just click in the Home checkbox.

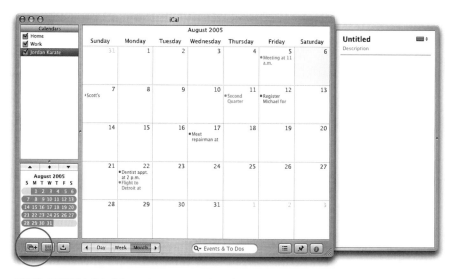

STEP SEVEN (Making Custom Calendars):
iCal gets really fun once you start adding your own custom calendars (other than the preset Home and Work calendars), so we're going to add another one. To add your own custom calendar, go under File and choose New Calendar. You can also click on the plus sign (+) in the bottom-left corner of the iCal window (it's technically called the Add a New Calendar button). When the new calendar appears in the Calendars list, type "Jordan Karate," then press the Return key. You'll notice the new calendar appears in red (the different colors help you keep track of your different calendars). You can add as many of these custom calendars as you'd like—just click on the plus sign button.

STEP EIGHT (Scheduling Events for a Custom Calendar):

Now, let's add Jordan's schedule for his karate classes to your calendar. Double-click in the white space on the 6th, type "10 a.m. grappling," and press the Return key (you'll notice that this entry also appears in red). On the 11th double-click and add "3:45 p.m. core class," and on the 22nd add "5 p.m. sparring" (you already have entries on those dates from other calendars, so double-click below all the other appointments to add new entries).

STEP NINE (Viewing Only Your Custom Calendar):
If you just want to see your son's karate schedule, in the Calendars list on
the left side of the iCal window, Option-Command click on the checkbox
to the left of the calendar's name, and you'll instantly see when your son's
karate classes are, as all other calendars are temporarily hidden from view.
(*Note:* To view all the calendars again, Command-click on any unselected
checkbox to the left of a calendar that's hidden.)

STEP TEN (Setting a Duration for an Event):

So far, we've been adding events that start at a certain time, but have no ending time. So, let's add one that has a set duration. In the Calendars list, click on Work, and then double-click in the white space on the 18th, type this event: "Vacation in Orlando," and press Return. Then, in the Info pane on the right side, click on the All-Day checkbox. (*Note:* If the Info pane isn't visible, press Command-I to toggle it on and off.) Where it says "From" and "To," go under the To section and click on the date, which will highlight. Now, type the date that you'll be coming back (in this case, you're coming back on Sunday the 21st, so type "21," then press the Return key). You'll see that a color bar now spans the length of your vacation, which is a great visual reminder not to plan something while you're on vacation.

STEP ELEVEN (Setting a Specific Event Time):

This works for hour durations as well (rather than just days), so double-click in the white space on the 23rd and add this event: "Lunch meeting at 12:30 at Applebee's." In the Info pane on the right, click once on the From time and type "12" for the hour, press Return, and type "30" for the minutes. Then, click once on the To time and type "3" for the hour, press Return, and type "00" for the minutes (hey, you're the boss—take a long lunch). Now click on the Day button at the bottom of the iCal window, and you can see how this appointment extends from 12:30 to 3 p.m., which helps you not to schedule anything else during that block of time.

STEP TWELVE (Setting an Alarm):

Back in Step 5, we added a 10 a.m. appointment on the 5th (and later changed it to 11 a.m.), right? To make sure you remember that appointment, we're going to set an alarm to remind you. First, repeat Step 11 to set your appointment to a specific time (from 11 a.m. to 12 p.m.). Then, click directly on that appointment on the 5th in your calendar. In the Info pane about halfway down, you'll see the word "Alarm." To set a reminder alarm, click once directly on the word "None," which appears to the right of the word "Alarm," and a pop-up menu of alarms will appear. You have a number of different choices, including having a message window pop up onscreen, having it pop up onscreen *and* sound a warning alert, or having iCal email you a reminder (among other things). For now, choose Message with Sound, and eventually a message window will appear onscreen to remind you, plus a sound will play to get your attention. Now, exactly when will this happen? That's up to you.

STEP THIRTEEN (Choosing Options for Your Alarm):

Once you choose an alarm, additional options will appear under the Alarm category. For example, when you choose Message with Sound, a pop-up menu appears in which you can choose a specific sound. Below that there's a pop-up menu for how many minutes, hours, or days before (or after) the event the message will appear. Click on the pop-up menus and choose your preferences.

ADDING A NEW ELEMENT OF FUN TO YOUR CALENDAR

TIP ▶ One of the coolest things about iCal is that you can subscribe to online calendars and have that information show up on your iCal calendar. For example, I'm a Tampa Bay Buccaneers fan, so every year I subscribe to a free Buc's NFL iCal calendar that adds all of that season's Bucs games (along with who they're playing and where) to my calendar. You'll be amazed at all the cool free calendars that are out there, and subscribing takes just one click. (Apple even has their own library of free iCal calendars you can subscribe to. You can find it online at www.apple.com/macosx/features/ical/library.)

3

Time

Goals

This lesson takes approximately 20 minutes to complete.

To import music into your Mac, download music from the Internet, and create a library of music. Then, organize your music into playlists and import this music into an Apple iPod MP3 player.

Playing Music on Your Mac (and Your iPod)

One of the coolest things about the Mac is how it handles music, especially when using your Mac with an Apple iPod MP3 player. The seamless way these two work together is just a beautiful thing to behold (and putting together and sorting your music collection is really a lot of fun. In fact, it's so much fun that compiling your library of songs can almost become a hobby of its own). The software we use to download, import, and organize music on a Mac is called iTunes. As powerful as iTunes is, it's amazingly easy to use, and having it sync with your iPod is even easier (the whole process is really pretty brilliant). iTunes lets you do three very important things: (1) It lets you import music from audio CDs (the same ones you buy at the record store in the mall); (2) it lets you buy and download music from the iTunes Music Store, which is the world's largest collection of legally downloadable music, with more than a million songs to choose from; and (3) it lets you organize all your music (no matter where it came from) into playlists that you create. Plus, if you have an iPod, a fourth iTunes feature appears, because when you connect an iPod to your Mac, iTunes copies your music playlists onto your iPod for you automatically. It all comes together to create one of the absolute most fun, most satisfying, and most exciting things about owning a Mac. Let's get to it!

STEP ONE (Setting Up iTunes):

Click once on the iTunes icon in the Dock on your desktop (its icon looks like a CD with a green music note on it). The first time you click on iTunes, the iTunes assistant window appears. It's going to ask you a few questions about how you want to set up iTunes. You can read each window and try to decide what to do, but for now I recommend just clicking the Next button in each window, which will basically leave all the settings as Apple recommends. Once you click Next three times, you're done, so click the Done button to close the iTunes assistant. When it closes, iTunes opens.

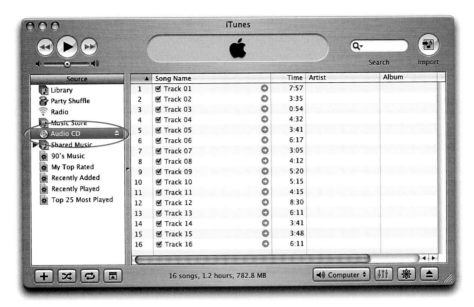

STEP TWO (Playing a Music CD, Part 1):

iTunes is essentially a music player, so to hear any music, you first have to get some music into it. You generally do this in one of two ways: (1) You import songs from a music CD, or (2) you download music from the Web (like from the iTunes Music Store, where you can *legally* buy and download music). We'll start with importing from a CD, so go grab a music CD and pop it in your Mac's CD (or DVD SuperDrive) drive. (I know, all your CDs are in your car. That's okay, I'll wait till you get back.) Okay, got a CD? Good. Pop it in the CD drive. In a few moments, this CD will appear in the Source list on the left side of the iTunes window.

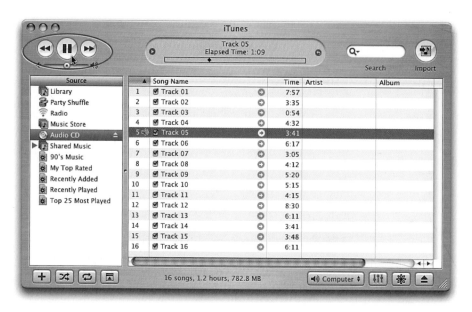

STEP THREE (Playing a Music CD, Part 2):

The songs on your CD will appear in the main window. (In fact, if you're connected to the Internet when you insert your CD, iTunes will quickly go to the Internet, find the names of the songs on your CD, and display the actual track names. If it can't find info on that particular CD, it will display the tracks as "Track 1," "Track 2," etc.) Well, although you technically haven't imported these songs into iTunes yet, you can play them (after all, iTunes is a music player, right?).

To play a song, press on it (in the main window), then click the Play button in the upper left-hand corner of the iTunes window. To stop the song from playing, click the Pause button (which switches from the Play button when a song is playing). You can also start or stop a song by pressing the Spacebar on your keyboard. To skip to the next song in the list, click the Next Song button (to the right of the Play button). To hear the previous track, click the Previous Song button (to the left of the Play button). To adjust the volume, drag the Volume slider (found directly below the Play button). *Note:* Even though you have a song selected, that doesn't mean it's the song that's playing. The small speaker icon to the left of the song name shows you which song is playing in the list. If you want to play a song that you have selected instead of the one that's playing now, just double-click on your selected song.

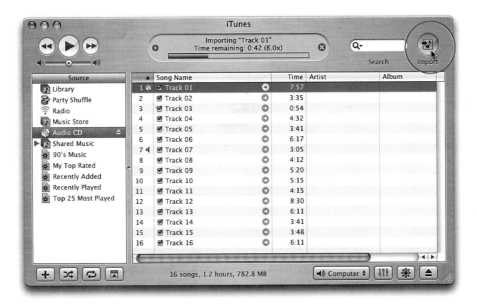

STEP FOUR (Importing Songs from Your CD):

You can play your CD in iTunes, but when you eject the CD, those songs are ejected right along with it. (By the way, to eject a CD, just click the little Eject icon that appears to the immediate right of the CD's name in the Source list. Don't do that now—I'm just mentioning it so you'll know how to later.)

So, before you eject the CD, you'll want to import those songs into iTunes. You do that by clicking the Import button in the top-right corner of the iTunes window. That's all you have to do—just click that button, and iTunes starts importing all the songs on that CD (actually, it imports all the songs that have a checkmark beside the name, so if there's a song you don't want to import, just click the checkmark to deselect it). If you look up at the status display in the top center of the iTunes window, it will read "Importing 'Name of Song.'" After a couple of minutes of importing, it will automatically start playing the imported songs starting with the first track (just in case you get bored waiting for all the songs to import). Once all the songs are imported (you'll know that they're imported because a green checkmark will appear beside the track number in the first column of each song, plus iTunes will alert you with a quick "dinging" sound), you can then eject the CD (by clicking that little icon I told you about earlier). Now you can take your CD and put it back in your car. Oh yeah, one more thing: Did you notice that when you ejected the CD the music keeps playing? That's because the music is now saved on your computer, playing in iTunes.

STEP FIVE (Accessing the iTunes Music Store):

Now that you know how to import songs from a CD, you're ready to download songs from the iTunes Music Store (it's simple, because there's a direct link between iTunes and the iTunes Music Store, so the process is pretty seamless). To visit the iTunes Music Store, you first have to be connected to the Internet, so make sure you're "online." (By the way, if you're not sure how to get online, check out Lesson 5 "Email and the Internet.") Once you're online, click on the words "Music Store" in the Source list (along the left side of the iTunes window). The home page of the iTunes Music Store will appear in your main window. You'll see lots of albums mentioned, and you can click on any of them to jump right to that album (almost everything you see is "clickable"), but instead of clicking on one of those, let's use one of my favorite features—the search (we'll actually do the searching in the next step).

STEP SIX (Finding Songs in the iTunes Music Store):

Let's start by searching for songs by the band U2. You do that by going to the Search Music Store field in the top-right corner of the iTunes window, typing "U2" in the field, and then pressing the Return key on your keyboard to begin the search. In just a few seconds, all the U2 songs available for download will be displayed. To hear a 30-second preview of any song, just double-click on it in the list (go ahead and double-click on one, like "Beautiful Day" or "Vertigo," which was used in one of Apple's TV ads for the iPod and the iTunes Music Store).

STEP SEVEN (Buying Songs):

If you decide you want to buy one of U2's songs, click the Buy Song button that appears to the far right of each song in the list (the price is listed to the left of the button. So far, songs sell for 99¢ each, but make sure you give the price a quick look in case it goes up or down in the future). When you click the Buy Song button, it asks you to sign in. If you already have an Apple account, you'll need to enter your Apple ID and Password. My guess is that you don't have one yet, but getting one is easy—just click the Create New Account button at the top of the window. It will take you through a sign-up process and form that's pretty much like every other sign-up form on the Web. You'll create a user name and password, and then you'll enter your name, address, etc., and info for the credit card you want to use for your song purchases. Once you've completed the form and gone through the process, you'll be automatically logged in, meaning you can start buying more songs (you won't have to fill out the form again—you now have an account).

STEP EIGHT (Viewing Your Downloaded Music):

Any songs you buy will appear in your song Library. To see the songs in your Library (which at this point are the songs you imported from the CD and any songs you bought from the iTunes Music Store), just click on Library in the Source list on the far left of the iTunes window. Now comes the fun part: sorting your music. You see, right now all your songs are listed in your Library (which is where your complete collection of songs—your library of music—is found). They're not grouped together or separated in any way—they're all just lumped together in one big list. So let's say the CD you imported was by the Black Eyed Peas. But let's say you also purchased songs (from the iTunes Music Store) by U2, David Bowie, The Hives, Green Day, and Norah Jones. These songs are all mixed in with your Black Eyed Peas songs in your Library. Well, I'm going to show you how to organize your songs in the next step.

STEP NINE (Organizing Your Music):

You can create order from this musical chaos by making playlists. For
example, you could create one for just your Black Eyed Peas songs, or for
dance music, or classic rock, etc. So, let's go ahead and create a playlist for
the CD you imported earlier. Click on the plus sign (+) button that appears
at the bottom-left corner of the iTunes window. This adds a new blank
playlist to the bottom of your Source list that's highlighted and ready for
you to name. So, type a name (use the name of the band whose songs you
imported from the CD) and press the Return key.

STEP TEN (Creating Playlists):

If you can't see your songs in the main window, click on Library in the Source list (so you can see your complete list of songs). Click on any one of the songs you imported from the CD, then press-and-hold the Command key on your keyboard (it's the key with the Apple logo on it) and click on each of the songs you imported from that album (or if the songs are contiguous, press-and-hold the Shift key and click on the first and last song from your CD in the list). When you get to the last song from your CD, release the Command (or Shift) key, and then click-and-hold—don't just click—on that last song and drag-and-drop it onto the new playlist you created in the Source list. As you drag, all the other songs you selected will come right along with the song you're dragging. As your cursor moves over your playlist, a little green plus sign (+) icon will appear below your cursor, which lets you know that you're adding songs to this playlist. Now release the mouse button and just those songs will appear in that playlist. If you want to add another song from your Library, just click on it, then drag-and-drop it onto that playlist. In the Source list, click on your new playlist and you'll see that it contains only the songs you selected. You can now start creating playlists and sorting your songs just the way you want them. By the way, to remove a song from a playlist, just click on it and press the Delete key on your keyboard (which removes the song from the playlist, not from your hard disk. To remove a song from your hard disk, click on it in your Library and press the Delete key).

STEP ELEVEN (Getting Music on Your iPod):

If you own an Apple iPod, it's time to take the show on the road. Once you've imported all the songs you want from your CDs and downloaded some music from the iTunes Music Store, you can easily transfer your songs (and your playlists) directly to your iPod, so you can listen to your songs wherever you go. All you have to do is connect your iPod to your Mac using the connector cable that came with your iPod. Depending on which iPod you own, you'll either have a USB or FireWire connector. (If you have an iPod Shuffle, just remove the cap from the bottom of the Shuffle and plug it directly into your Mac's USB port.) To connect your iPod, plug one end of the connector into the bottom of your iPod and the other end into the matching slot on your Mac. Then, iTunes will automatically transfer your playlists and songs to your iPod. You don't have to do anything—it's completely automatic—just connect your iPod and iTunes does the rest. (*Note:* That sounds too easy, eh? Well, the only other thing you have to do is make sure your iPod's software is already installed on your computer and it's up to date. So, you may need to go to Apple.com and download the latest iPod software.) When the all songs are transferred to your iPod, you can remove your iPod, plug in your earphones, and hear the music from your playlists. If you download new songs, import new songs, create new playlists, etc., everything will automatically be updated to reflect your changes when you reconnect your iPod. Sweet!

4

Time

Goals

This lesson takes approximately 30 minutes to complete.

To import photos from your digital camera, then view, edit, crop, and print them using Apple's iPhoto application.

Getting Photos into Your Mac (Viewing, Editing, and Printing)

Digital photography has changed the way we use our cameras, and important as the digital camera is, without a computer to view and edit those photos, the digital photography revolution never would've happened. Luckily, Mac OS X Tiger was built with digital photographers in mind, and it comes with an amazing application called iPhoto that lets you import, organize, print, and share your photos, all in a very intuitive, fun way. Also, because of the way Macs are designed, getting your digital photos into your computer is a breeze. That's because most of today's digital cameras come with a USB cable that lets you connect your camera directly to your Mac (if yours didn't come with that cable, or you can't find your cable, you can buy a digital memory card reader for as little as ten bucks online or from your local camera store). That's all you need to enter the world of sorting, editing, and printing your digital camera photos on your Mac. In this lesson, we'll look at how to import photos, create a slide show using your photos, edit and crop your photos, share them, print them, and just about anything else you want to do with photos—and we're going to do all that within one brilliant little application called iPhoto.

STEP ONE (Connecting Your Camera to Your Mac):

When you bought your digital camera, chances are it came with a USB connector cable so you can transfer photos from your camera to your computer. If for some reason you can't find your cable (or your camera didn't have one from the start), you could buy a replacement cable. However, I recommend that you instead buy an inexpensive memory card reader (you can find digital camera memory card readers at Apple.com, the Apple Store, or wherever digital cameras are sold). Here's how they work: You turn off your digital camera, eject your memory card from your camera, and then slide your memory card into your card reader. You then take the card's USB connector and insert it into your Mac's USB port. Once you do this, your Mac will instantly recognize that you've connected a digital camera (or memory card reader). Automatically, iPhoto will launch (the application we use to import, organize, edit, and print photos) so you can begin importing your photos. Likely, this is your first time launching iPhoto, so you'll see a Welcome screen pop up asking if you want to use iPhoto as your default image editor. Click the Use iPhoto button, and the iPhoto interface will appear.

STEP TWO (Importing Photos from Your Digital Camera):
When iPhoto appears, it knows you have a digital camera connected, so it's
ready to import your photos, and to let you know that it displays a large icon
of a digital camera in the center of its main window (as shown above). It will
also let you know how many photos it finds on your camera's memory card
by telling you it's ready to import X number of photos. All you have to do to
import those photos (from your digital camera into iPhoto) is click on the
Import button in the bottom right-hand corner of iPhoto's window (see, I told
you this was easy), but *don't* click it just yet.

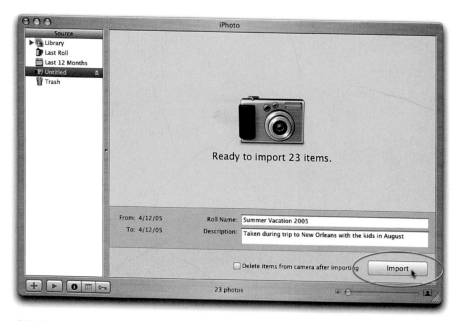

STEP THREE (Organizing Your Photos Before You Import):
Before you click the Import button, to help you keep things organized, I
recommend clicking in the Roll Name field near the bottom of iPhoto's
window and typing a name for this roll of "digital film" (for example, you
might name this roll "Summer Vacation 2005"). Then, click in the Description
field directly below it and type a brief description (for example, "Taken during
trip to New Orleans with the kids in August"). Now, click the Import button to
bring your photos into iPhoto.

TO DO OR NOT TO DO: AUTO-ERASING YOUR PHOTOS

TIP ▶ iPhoto is set up so that once you turn on the checkbox that
reads "Delete items from camera after importing" (which appears at the
bottom of the iPhoto window), iPhoto will delete your images from
your digital memory card. If you *don't* want iPhoto to erase your original
photos, ensure that checkbox is turned off; if you *do* want iPhoto to empty
your memory card, click on the checkbox to select it. When you have this
option turned on, a warning will pop up ensuring that you want to delete
your original image files—just to double check that's what you really
want to do.

STEP FOUR (Disconnecting Your Camera or Memory Card Reader):
Once you've imported your photos, you no longer need to have your digital camera or memory card reader attached to your computer. If you look in the Source list on the left side of iPhoto, you'll see your camera listed by name (if iPhoto doesn't recognize your camera's name, it appears as "Untitled"). To eject your camera (or card reader), just click on the little Eject icon that appears to the far right of its name (it's circled above). It's now safe to remove the USB connector cable from your Mac.

HOW TO STOP IMPORTING (AND OTHER IMPORTANT INFO)

TIP If you're importing hundreds of photos, it can take a while, so if at any point you decide you want to stop the import process, just click on the Stop Import button in the bottom-right corner of iPhoto's window. Also, don't disconnect your camera's (or reader's) cable while importing; otherwise, you'll risk damaging the photos on your memory card. If you need to disconnect, click the Stop Import button first, then eject the memory card as shown above. Oh, and one other thing: If your camera has a sleep mode (meaning it shuts itself off when it's idle), you'll need to turn that off, because if your camera goes to sleep while iPhoto is importing images, it can disrupt the import process.

STEP FIVE (Viewing Your Imported Photos):

Once your photos are imported, you'll see small versions of photos displayed in iPhoto's main window (these small versions of your photos are called "thumbnails"). You can change the size of these thumbnails by clicking-and-dragging on the slider in the bottom right-hand corner of iPhoto's window (shown circled above). Click-and-drag the slider to the right to make the thumbnails larger; drag to the left to make them smaller (making them smaller makes more of them visible, since they take up less space onscreen). Depending on how many photos you import, all of them may not be visible onscreen at once. If that's the case, a scroll bar will appear on the right side of the iPhoto window (it looks like a blue pill-shaped bar). With your mouse, click-and-drag that blue bar up or down to display the rest of your photos.

ROTATING PHOTOS

TIP ▸ If you need to rotate a photo (you took the photo with your camera turned vertically), first click on the photo thumbnail in the iPhoto window that you want to rotate, then click the Rotate button, found just below all your thumbnails on the bottom-left side of the iPhoto window. It will rotate counterclockwise by default, so keep clicking the button until the photo is in the proper orientation (landscape or portrait).

STEP SIX (Editing Your Photos for Contrast and Color):

One of the most amazing things about iPhoto is the power it has to let you fix problem photos (i.e., photos that are too light, too dark, slightly blurry, lacking contrast, have "red eye," etc.) and enhance photos (by adding sepia tone effects, converting them to black and white for dramatic effect, cropping your images for maximum impact, and a host of other things that take your photos from flat to fabulous). The process of enhancing or fixing your photos is called "editing." This editing is done in a separate window that displays your photos at a larger size (helpful when editing). To edit a photo, just double-click directly on its thumbnail and it will open in iPhoto's editing window. At the bottom of this editing window is a row of buttons, and each performs a different photo fix. Perhaps the most popular is the Enhance button. By clicking this button once, iPhoto adjusts the color and contrast of your photo, often with amazingly good results. So double-click on one of your photos that looks kind of flat and lifeless, and then click this Enhance button to see for yourself (as I did here). *Note:* After you've clicked Enhance, you can see a before-and-after preview by pressing the Control key (it's on the far left on your keyboard) a few times.

CROPPING PHOTOS

TIP To crop a photo in the editing window, just take your mouse and click-and-drag over the area you want to keep. Then, click on the Crop button at the bottom center of the editing window. You can reposition your cropping area by clicking inside it and dragging with your mouse. To cancel your crop, click outside the cropping box and it will disappear.

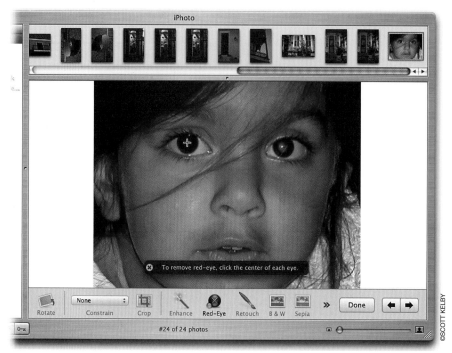

©SCOTT KELBY

STEP SEVEN (Removing Red Eye):

One of the other digital photography problems you're likely to face is the dreaded "red eye" (where the person's eyes appear red in the photo, which is caused by the flash being too close to the lens, among other things). If you have a photo where the subject has red eye, double-click on the photo's thumbnail to open it in the editing window. Zoom into your image by clicking-and-dragging the slider (in the bottom-right corner of the editing window) to the right. Then, click on the Red-Eye button in the bottom center of the editing window. (*Note:* If you don't see the tool in the bottom of the window, click-and-hold on the double right-facing arrows until a menu appears, and then choose Red-Eye from the list.) Your cursor will change to a crosshair, so click with your mouse over each eye, and in seconds the red eye will be gone. Once you're finished, click on the X in the top-left corner of the red-eye box along the bottom of your photo.

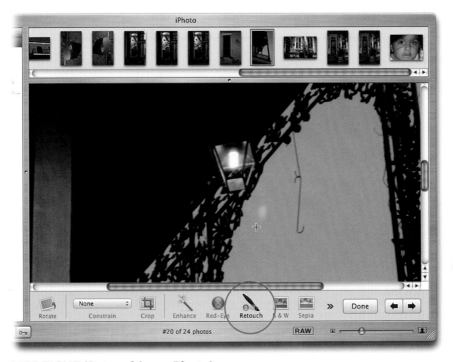

STEP EIGHT (Retouching a Photo):

There are other changes you can apply in this editing window, including one-click buttons for converting your photo to black and white or to a sepia tone (which applies an orangey tint to your photo). There's also a retouching brush, which lets you remove spots, specks, blemishes, acne, and other little stuff that needs removing. To use the retouching brush, click on the Retouch button, and once your cursor changes to a crosshair, click on the blemish, mole, wart, speck, etc., that you want to retouch. It may actually take a few clicks before it's gone. *Note:* You may need to zoom into your image, so click-and-drag on the slider in the bottom-right corner of the editing window. Then, position your image onscreen using the scroll bars that appear along the bottom and to the right of your image.

WHEN YOU'RE DONE EDITING

TIP When you're done editing your photo and you want to return to the main window (where all your thumbnails are), just click the Done button in the bottom-right side of the editing window.

STEP NINE (Creating an Album):

When your photos are first imported into iPhoto, they're imported into your main Library with all your other photos (in other words, all your photos are stored in one big list, which is somewhat similar to throwing all your prints into one big shoebox—it makes finding the photos you want quite a chore). Luckily, iPhoto lets you sort and organize your photos using "albums" (just like you would with regular prints). For example, let's look at what we used to do before digital: You'd return from your vacation, get your prints developed, sort the good shots from the bad ones, and then you'd put the good ones in a photo album. Well, you're going to do the same thing in iPhoto—you're just doing it all on your computer. To create an album, click on the plus sign (+) button that appears in the bottom-left corner of the iPhoto window (it's circled above). A little window will pop down from the top of iPhoto asking you to name your new album, so just type a name (let's say you went on that New Orleans vacation we mentioned earlier, and now you're going to use this album to separate the good shots from the bad, so name this album "New Orleans") and click on the Create button. This new album will appear in the Source list on the left side of iPhoto.

STEP TEN (Using Albums):

In the Source list on the left side of iPhoto, click on the word "Library" to display all your imported photos. It's now time to start sorting. When you find a photo you like (one that you might put in a traditional photo album), click on it, then drag-and-drop it right onto your New Orleans album (that appears in the Source list on the left). As you move your mouse over the New Orleans album, you'll see that familiar little green icon with a plus sign beneath your arrow cursor letting you know you're about to add something to that album (and that's exactly what you want to do). Also, the album will have a black highlight bar around it to let you know that it's selected. When you release your mouse button, you won't see anything happen onscreen, but as long as you saw that little green plus sign icon appear at the bottom of your arrow cursor, you can rest assured that the photo you just dragged is really in that album. If you want to be sure, just click once on the New Orleans album and you'll see this album only contains that one photo you just dragged. (By the way, to get back to your Library, just click on the word "Library" in the Source list on the left side of iPhoto.) Well, believe it or not, that's how easy creating albums is—you just drag-and-drop your favorite photos from your Library right into your album, and when you're done, click on the album to see what's inside (just your best photos). So go ahead and do this for your new album.

STEP ELEVEN (Putting Your Photos in Order):

Okay, so now the best photos (your "keepers") are in their own album. That's good, but they're probably not in the exact order you'd like them, right? Well, don't worry, because now that they're in an album, you can put them in the exact order you want by simply clicking on a photo and dragging it into the position you want. That's it—drag 'em where you want 'em. As you drag a photo, you'll see a little "ghost" version of the photo so you know exactly where it's going as you drag it. Also, as you drag your "ghosted" photo between two existing photo thumbnails, you'll see a thin vertical bar appear, letting you know that if you release the mouse button now, that's where your photo will appear (positioned between those two photos). Try it once and you'll instantly see what I mean.

STEP TWELVE (Creating Slide Shows):

Want to see a full-screen slide show of the photos in your New Orleans album? Start by ensuring that no photos are selected in the iPhoto window (meaning none of your photos have a blue outline around them). Now click on the Slideshow button at the bottom of the iPhoto window (its icon looks like two slides stacked on top of each other). This takes you to a window where you can decide how your slide show will look, what kind of music will accompany your slide show, and how it will appear as it transitions between photos. To take a quick peek at how your slide show will look using Apple's default settings, just click the Play button on the left side of the iPhoto window. Your screen will go black for a moment, then your first photo will fill your entire screen, while acoustic guitar music plays in the background. Your photo will be panning slowly across your screen, and in a few seconds, your second photo will softly dissolve into view and pan in a different direction (perhaps it will slowly zoom toward you). This slow dissolving and panning will continue through all the photos in your New Orleans album, and it will repeat over and over until you press the Escape (Esc) key on your keyboard.

STOPPING THE PANNING MOVEMENT

TIP The slow panning and zooming that is applied to your slide show is called the Ken Burns Effect. If you want to turn it off, just click on the Settings button, and when the pop-down window appears, turn off the checkbox for Automatic Ken Burns Effect. Also, if you can't see the buttons along the bottom of the window, either click on the double right-facing arrows and choose your settings from the menu that appears or click on the corner of the main iPhoto window and drag it to the right to extend it across your screen.

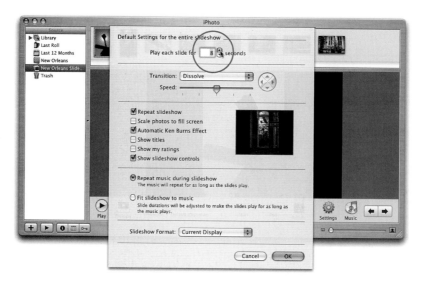

STEP THIRTEEN (Editing Your Slide Show):

Once you click the Slideshow button, thumbnails of the photos in your album appear across the top of the iPhoto window. These are there so you can sort the photos that appear in your slide show. You sort them here the same way you do in the regular thumbnail window—click on thumbnails, then drag-and-drop them into the order you want them. Also, if you click the Settings button at the bottom of the iPhoto window, a pop-down window will appear, in which you have an assortment of options. At the top of the window, you can choose how many seconds each photo will display onscreen before the next photo appears. To change the number of seconds, either type a number in the field or click on the little arrow buttons (circled above)—click the Up Arrow to add seconds or the Down Arrow to lessen the time they're onscreen. Just below that, you can decide how the photos will appear as one photo gives way to the next by selecting an effect from the Transition pop-up menu. You can also choose how long that transition will take using the Speed slider that appears just below the Transition pop-up menu.

CONTROLLING THE SLIDE SHOW ONCE IT'S RUNNING

TIP ▶ If you want to have control over your slide show once it's running (like pause it, see the previous/next photo, etc.), before you click the Play button, click the Settings button. When the Settings window appears, turn on the checkbox for Show Slideshow Controls. Now click Play, and controls will appear onscreen for you.

STEP FOURTEEN (Adding Music to Your Slide Show):

As I mentioned earlier, Apple has already picked some background music for you that will play with your slide show when you click the Play button (that's a good thing, because background music makes a world of difference in photo slide shows). However, if you've imported music into your Mac (from CDs or downloaded from the iTunes Music Store), you can use one of those songs as your background music instead. Here's how: First, click the Music button (it's circled above), which brings up a window onscreen showing all the playlists of music you have in your iTunes Library. You can click on any playlist, and the songs in that playlist will play, in order, as your background music. However, if there's just one song you want to use, and you know the name of the song, you can instead use the Search field located along the bottom center of the window. Just click on Library in the top list in the window, and then click inside the Search field. Start typing the name of the song in the field, and if it's in your iTunes Library, it will appear in the Song list. You can just click on the song to select it, and then click the OK button.

TURNING OFF THE BACKGROUND MUSIC

TIP ▶ If you decide you don't want background music for your slide show, just click the Music button in the bottom-right corner of the iPhoto window. When the slide show music options appear, turn off the checkbox at the top that says "Play music during slideshow," and then click the OK button.

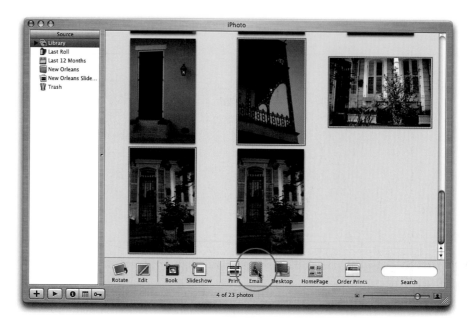

STEP FIFTEEN (Emailing a Photo, Part 1):

If you have a particular photo you want to email (or even a group of photos), you can start the process right within iPhoto. First, click on the Library in the Source list along the left side of the iPhoto window. Then, click on the photo that you want to email (or if there's more than one photo you want to email, click on the first photo, then hold the Command key [the key with the Apple logo on it], and click on the other photos you want to email). With your photo(s) selected, click the Email button in the bottom of the iPhoto window (its icon looks like a postage stamp).

STEP SIXTEEN (Emailing a Photo, Part 2):
The Mail Photo dialog will appear asking how large you want your photos to be. The default size is Medium, which is 640 pixels wide by 480 pixels deep (that's a standard size for viewing photos onscreen, so that size is almost ideal for emailing). You can choose a larger size if you're just emailing one or two photos, but if you're emailing more than that, it's best to keep the Size set to Medium (640x480). Now, click the blue Compose button, and iPhoto will compress your photos (for fast emailing).

STEP SEVENTEEN (Emailing a Photo, Part 3):

Once the photos are compressed, Apple's Mail program will launch automatically and attach the photo(s) you choose to an email document. All you have to do is type the email address of the person you're sending the photos to, then press the Tab key on your keyboard twice so the Subject field is highlighted (iPhoto will already have inserted a generic subject line). Now you can type a subject line (maybe something like "Here are the shots we took in New Orleans," provided, of course, that you did take these photos in New Orleans. If these are shots you took in Utah, you should probably type that instead). If you want to add a message, click in the message area, press the Return key a few times, then press the Up Arrow key on your keyboard a few times to add a some space between your photos and your message. Type your message, and when you're finished, click the Send button in the top-left corner of the message window to email your photos.

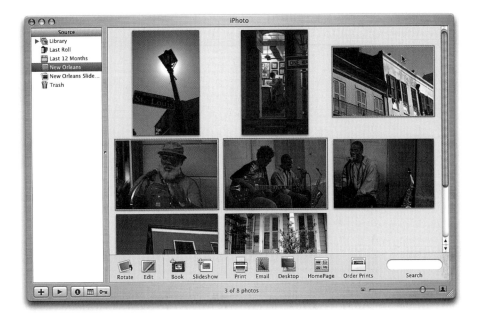

STEP EIGHTEEN (Printing Your Photos, Part 1):

Before you begin to print, you first must select the images you want to print. You can click on an album in the Source list (meaning you want to print the entire album). However, if you want to print specific photos, you can press the Command key (it has the Apple logo on it) and click on the individual photos in the main window that you want to print. You can select photos from your Library or from an album; it's up to you. With your images selected, you now have three choices when it comes to printing your photos. We'll discuss these in the next few steps.

STEP NINETEEN (Printing Your Photos, Part 2):
Your first choice is printing to your color printer. Of course, you need to
have a color printer connected to your Mac to do this. If you do, click the
Print button at the bottom center of iPhoto's window. When the print options
appear, choose your printer (by its name) from the top pop-up menu, choose
what size prints you want (Full Page, Greeting Card, etc.) from the Style pop-
up menu, how many copies you want of each photo, and then click the blue
Print button.

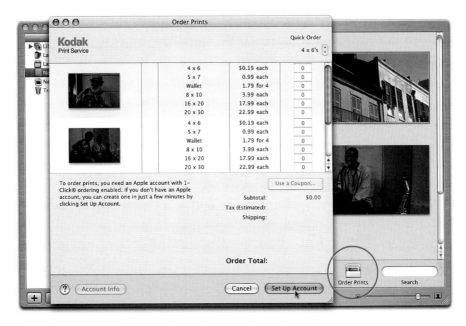

STEP TWENTY (Printing Your Photos, Part 3):

You can send your photos directly to Kodak's Print Service, right from iPhoto, and they'll print and mail them directly to you (just like a regular photo lab). To do this, ensure you've selected the photos you want to print (which we did in Step 18), and then click the Order Prints button near the bottom-right corner of iPhoto's window. This will take you to an order window, in which you can choose sizes, quantities, etc. But first, you'll need to click on the Set Up Account button and go through the steps it provides to set up an account with Kodak Print Service (which uses your Apple .Mac account, if you have one). Once your account is active, you can make your selections for each photo you want to print.

STEP TWENTY-ONE (Printing Your Photos, Part 4):

You can send your photos to Apple to have a hardcover photo book made just for you. These books are absolutely amazing, and surprisingly affordable. To get an idea of how amazing, click on your New Orleans album in the Source list (this selects those photos, though nothing happens onscreen), then click the Book button near the bottom-left side of the iPhoto window. This brings up options with a list of styles on the left. Click on the style you want, choose the book size you want from the pop-up menu at the top of the window, and then click the Choose Theme button. When the iPhoto window shows your book layout options, click the Autoflow button in the bottom of the iPhoto window (if you can't see it, click on the double right-facing arrows and choose Autoflow from the menu that appears). Now, sit back and prepare to be amazed.

5

Time

Goals

This lesson takes approximately 15 minutes to complete.

To configure your Mac to give you email access and Web access, so you can send and receive email and search the World Wide Web.

Email and the Internet

My guess is that the ability to send email and get on the Internet are two of the main reasons why you bought a Mac in the first place. (Okay, they're probably the reasons why you bought a computer—but you bought a Macintosh computer because it's more fun, easier to use, more reliable, and you wanted to avoid all those icky things that PC users wrestle with every day, like viruses and spyware. Right? Right.) Well, my friends, you did the right thing, and you'll know that for sure, because in just a few minutes, you'll be doing both of those things: sending and receiving email *and* surfing the Web (even though the term "surfing" as it relates to the Web is so overplayed that we don't really use it anymore. We'll just say we're "on the Web" and leave it at that). Now, the first step to getting on the Web (and sending email) happens before you even start up your Mac. Basically, you need to find a provider (usually your phone company, your local cable TV provider, or an Internet service like AOL or Earthlink) that will allow you access to the Internet, so you'll need to do that first, before you even start this lesson. If you can get high-speed Internet access, do it—you will love it—everything happens so quickly. It makes the Internet an entirely different experience, as opposed to the otherwise slow and sometimes frustrating world of using your regular phone line (called "dial up") to access the Internet. But the important thing is that you get access to the Internet (basically a user name and a password) before you go any further. Once you have those handy, you're ready to get "on the Web."

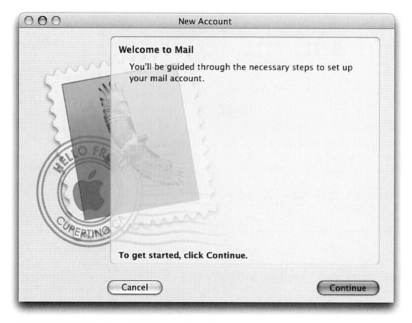

STEP ONE (Setting Up Your Email Account):

We'll start with setting up your email account. Mac OS X Tiger comes with a wonderful application for sending, receiving, and managing your email. It's called (are you ready for this?) Mail. Okay, it's not a particularly cool name, but the program itself is actually very cool, and very well designed. To launch Mail, go ahead and click on the Mail icon in the Dock (its icon looks like a blue postage stamp with a bird on it). The first time you launch Mail, a window pops up to take you through the process of setting up your email account (basically, this is where you'll enter the user name, password, and other settings provided by your Internet Service Provider [we call it your ISP]).

STUFF YOU'LL BE ASKED VERY SOON, AND NEED TO KNOW

TIP ▶ When setting up your Mac to send and receive email, you're going to be asked for five bits of information that you'll need to get from the company that's providing your Internet access. You'll need to ask your ISP these things: (1) What type of account do I have? (Is it a POP account or an IMAP account?) (2) What is my user name? (3) What is my password? (4) What is my email address? (5) What is my Incoming (and Outgoing) Mail Server? Mail will ask for all five, so when you set up your Internet account, find out the answers to all five questions, write them down, and have them handy.

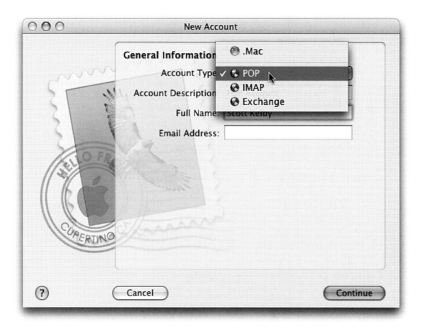

STEP TWO (Entering Some General Information):

Once you click the Continue button in the first screen (the Welcome screen), it asks for general information about your email account. If you've signed up for Apple's handy .Mac service, you'll get a .Mac email address, and you can enter that information here. You enter your user name and password in the User Name and Password fields (I know, that was kind of obvious), and you're pretty much done. However, if you don't have a .Mac account, meaning your Internet Service Provider set you up with an email account, you've got a little work to do. First, you'll need to choose your type of account. Click on the down-facing arrow to the right of the words "Account Type" and a pop-up menu will appear (it shows .Mac by default). This is where it asks the first question I mentioned in the TIP on the facing page, and that is do you have a POP account or an IMAP account? Choose the one you were told you had from this pop-up menu (chances are it's a POP account, so we'll continue along those lines). Where it says Account Description, you can use any description you like (such as AOL Internet, Earthlink Account, etc.). Where it says Full Name, type your name. Where it says Email Address (do I even have to tell you this one?). Okay, that's the first screen, now click the blue Continue button.

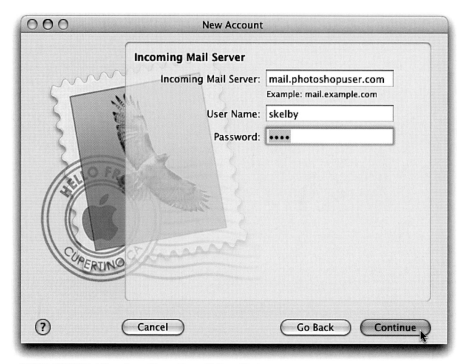

STEP THREE (Getting Your Email Set Up):
The next screen asks you for information on your Incoming Mail Server.
Again, this is one of those "five important things" that I mentioned earlier that
you'll need to find out from your ISP when you set up your account. Type that
information in the Incoming Mail Server field (see, I told you you'd be asked
for this stuff—that's why it pays to have it handy *before* you start setting up the
Mail application). Once you've entered the Incoming Mail Server info, press the
Tab key on your keyboard to jump to the User Name field. Again, enter the user
name given to you by your ISP, then press the Tab key once more to jump to the
Password field and enter your password. Now click the blue Continue button.

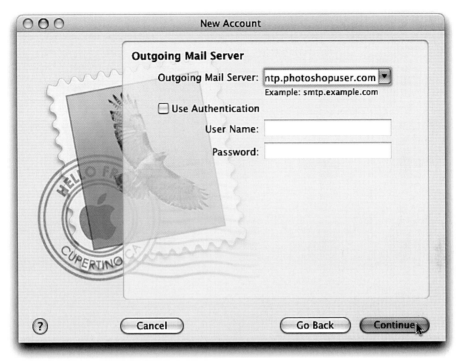

STEP FOUR (Setting Up Your Mail Server):
The next setup screen is the Incoming Mail Security screen, which requires
a password for authentication of your incoming email. That's fine for now, so
just click the blue Continue button to move on to the next screen, which is the
Outgoing Mail Server. Again, here you'll enter more info given to you by your
Internet Service Provider. The Outgoing Mail Server info is sometimes referred
to as "SMTP info." Look on your list of things you asked your ISP, and enter
the SMTP information in the first field. For now, you can skip the section for
using authentication for outgoing mail, so click the blue Continue button.

STEP FIVE (Reviewing Your Information):
You can also skip the Outgoing Mail Security screen that appears next, so click the Continue button again. The next screen that appears is just a summary of the information you've already entered (as shown above), so you can look that over and just click the Continue button one more time. That's it—you've created a new email account, so click the blue Done button that appears on the final screen. You're now ready to send and receive email.

STEP SIX (Sending an Email):

Now that you've completed the setup, the Mail application opens automatically. We'll start by sending an email, so click the New button, which appears along the top of the Mail window (it's just right of center). When you click this button, a new email message window appears. In the To field, type the email address of the person you want to receive this email. If you want to send a carbon copy of this email to someone else, press the Tab key on your keyboard to jump to the Cc field, and then type his or her email address. Press the Tab key to jump to the Subject field. This field is important, because when your friend receives your email, what's written in this Subject field is what he'll see in his email application, so type a subject. Now press the Tab key one more time so your cursor is in the message area.

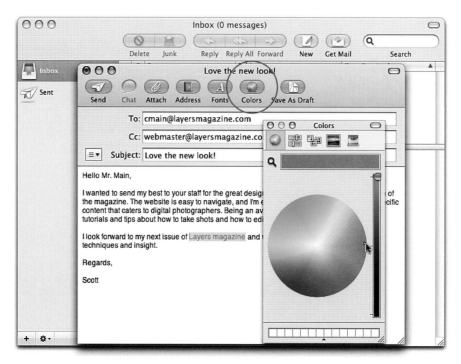

STEP SEVEN (Customizing Your Text):

Now you can start typing your message, just like you would a regular letter. You can choose the font (typeface) your email message will appear in by clicking on the Fonts button in the top center of the New Message window. This brings up the Font dialog, in which you can choose the font, style (bold, italic, etc.), and size you want. To change the color of one or more words, just click-and-drag your cursor over the words that you want to colorize to highlight them, then click the Colors button (to the right of the Fonts button). When the Colors dialog appears, click on the color you want in the color wheel, then click on the first round button in the top left of the Colors dialog to close it.

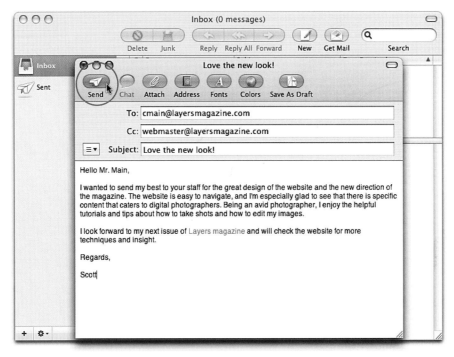

STEP EIGHT (Sending Your Email):

When you're done typing your message, all you have to do to send the email to your friend is click the Send button at the top of the New Message window (it's the first button from the left). In a few moments you'll hear a swoosh sound (that's a technical term) to let you know that your email has been sent.

STEP NINE (Getting Email):

Once you give out your email address to friends, family, co-workers, etc., it won't be long before you start getting email yourself. When you launch Mail, it automatically checks for any new mail, but you can check manually anytime by clicking the Get Mail button located at the top of the interface, just to the right of the New button. When mail arrives for you, it will appear in the Mail window with a blue dot to the left of it (that blue dot indicates that this email has not been read yet). You'll also see the name of the person who sent the mail, the email's subject, and when this email was received. To read an email, just click on it once and the email message will be displayed in the lower portion of Mail's main window.

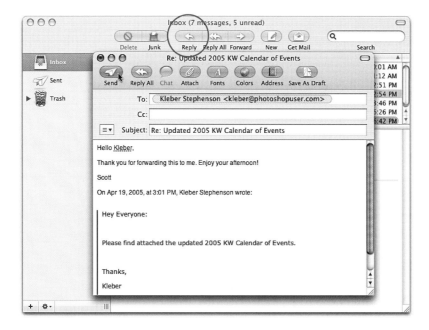

STEP TEN (Replying to Email):

Once you've read an email, if you decide you want to respond to the person who emailed you, just click the Reply button at the top center of the Mail interface (its icon is a left-facing arrow). This automatically puts the email address of the person who emailed you into the To field, and it adds the word "Re:" in front of the subject line, so the person who gets this email reply from you knows that you're referring to the original email sent to you (in other words, the person will instantly know it's your reply). Another benefit of clicking the Reply button is Mail includes the original email directly below where you're going to type your response, so the person doesn't have to remember exactly what he wrote you—instead he can scroll down to see the original email below your reply. Again, you have the same control here over fonts and colors as you do with a regular email message. When you're done typing your reply, just click the Send button in the top-left corner of the New Message window, and your reply will be sent.

DELETING UNWANTED EMAIL

TIP If you get an email you don't want (like some junk email, commonly referred to as "spam"), you can delete it by clicking once on the email in the main Mail window, and then either click the Delete button in the top left of the interface or press the Delete key on your keyboard.

STEP ELEVEN (Emailing Photos):

Besides just emailing text, you can attach a file to your email as well, and photos are one of the most popular files to attach to an email. Luckily, emailing a photo is a breeze in Mac OS X Tiger. Start by clicking on any empty space on your desktop to switch to the Finder (any empty space surrounding the Mail interface will do). Now double-click directly on your Macintosh HD icon to display a window showing the contents of your Mac's hard disk. Click once on the Pictures folder that appears along the left side of that window. Clicking on that icon displays the photos that are stored in your Pictures folder. Find the photo you want to include with your email, then click-and-drag that photo directly onto the Mail icon down in the Dock. Mail will open a New Message window for you, and you'll see your photo appear in the body of the email message.

STEP TWELVE (Sending Text with Your Photo):
Now all you have to do is enter the email address of the person you want
to send the photo to in the To field and enter a topic in the Subject field. If
you want to include an email note with your photo, click once to the right
of your photo, press the Return key two times, then press the Up Arrow key
on your keyboard twice. Now, start typing your note. When you're done
with your message, click the Send button in the top-left corner of the New
Message window, and your email, along with the photo, will be sent. By the
way, you can attach more than one photo to an email—just press-and-hold the
Command key (the one with the Apple logo on it) and click on all the photos
you want to email. Then, click-and-drag any one to the Mail icon in the Dock
and all the others will come along with it, but don't send too many photos (not
more than 5 megabytes) or your recipient's email account might reject your
email for being too large.

STEP THIRTEEN (Getting "on the Web"):

Now that you've sent some email, it's time to explore the Web, which is your online destination for everything from news, weather, and sports to online shopping, research, entertainment, and just plain fun. To get on the Web, you first have to be connected to the Internet, so go ahead and connect to the Internet using the method recommended by your Internet Service Provider (probably with a cable modem, DSL, or dial up using a telephone line and your internal modem). Once you're connected, to visit a website you'll use Safari, Apple's Web browser, so click on the Safari icon in the Dock to launch it (its icon looks like a blue compass). This opens your Web browser and takes you to a startup page created by Apple.

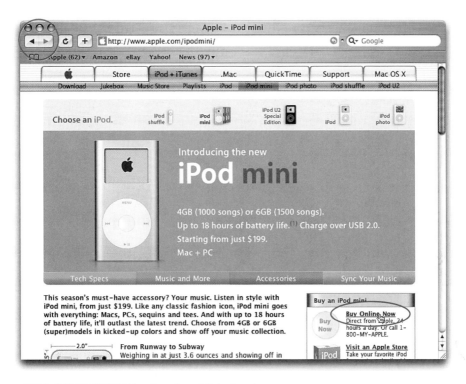

STEP FOURTEEN (Navigating Websites):

On websites (like this one, for example), you can learn more about anything you see on the page by either: (a) clicking on any text underlined in blue (called a link), or (b) clicking on any photo that has a link embedded. For example, if you see a photo of Apple's iPod somewhere on the page, and you click on the photo, it will likely take you to a page with information on the iPod. Although most photos on websites are live "links" to other webpages, you can easily find out which photos (and text) have links by simply moving your mouse over a particular photo (or text). If your cursor changes from a black arrow to a hand pointing upward—that's a link; so if you click your mouse when your cursor shows the pointing hand, your browser will jump to that page. To get back to the previous page (the page where you originally clicked), click the Back button (which is the left-facing arrow in the top-left corner of your browser window). To get to a subsequent page, click the Next button (it's the right-facing arrow in the top-left corner).

STEP FIFTEEN (Finding Things on the Web):

Okay, so you found Apple's webpage, but how do you find other websites? You search for them, and you can do that right within Safari, as there's a search field in the top right-hand corner of Safari's window that lets you search using the hottest Web search engine on the planet—Google. To search for a site, you just have to click your mouse once in the Google field, and type the word you're searching for. For example, if you want to find webpages that have information on Nikon cameras, just type the word "Nikon" in the Google field, then press the Return key on your keyboard. In just seconds, Google gives you a list of all the sites it found that contain information about Nikon, and they're listed by order of relevance, so naturally the first link it lists is Nikon's own website. To jump directly to that site, just click on the blue underlined link that reads "Nikon USA." Other sites are listed below where you can learn more or buy Nikon cameras (the site links listed on the right side of the window are paid links, so these are usually sites that sell products).

NARROW YOUR SEARCH

TIP ▶ Now, if you want to be more specific and search for a digital camera, and you type it as *digital camera*, you'll get search results that show every site that contains the word "digital" or the word "camera." In my search, that produced more than 49 million sites. So, to narrow your search, put quotes around the entire phrase (as in "digital camera"), and then Google will search for that exact phrase—digital camera—and not the word "digital," then the word "camera."

STEP SIXTEEN (If You Know Where You Want to Go):

If you know the name of the website you want to visit, all you have to do is click three times in the long, center field at the top of the browser to highlight all the text that's already there, then type the Web address you want to go to. For example, if you wanted to visit the website for the publisher of this book (which is Peachpit Press), you can just type the word "Peachpit" in the main address window that runs across the top of your browser window and press the Return key (technically, Peachpit's Web address is www.peachpit.com, but if you just type in a single name like this, Safari assumes that it's a ".com" so it adds that information for you automatically. Another example: If you want to visit CNN.com, you can just type "CNN" (without the quotes). You don't need to type "www" or that "http://" thing—just type "CNN," press Return, and in a second or two, you're there.

TYPING A WEB ADDRESS

TIP If you're going to type a Web address, you first have to erase the address of the current website that's displayed in the main address bar that runs across the top of your browser. Instead of clicking three times, how about clicking only once? Simply click on the tiny icon that appears before the Web address that's there now and the entire Web address will highlight for you. Now all you have to do is start typing and the new Web address you're typing will automatically erase the address that was previously there.

STEP SEVENTEEN (Getting Back to Places You've Been):

Okay, so let's say you found a website you really like (maybe it's a site that offers airline discounts), and you want to be able to visit here again when it's time for your next trip. You don't have to memorize or write down the location of this website, instead you can "bookmark it" so you can jump right back there anytime with just one click. Here's how: When you're at that travel site, go under the Bookmarks menu (at the very top of your screen) and choose Add Bookmark. This brings up a small window asking you to name your bookmark (you can use the name already provided by the site, but if it's too long, you might want to create your own). Then, click once on the words "Bookmarks Bar" and you'll see a list of categories in which you can save this bookmark. Apple has already created a folder called Travel, and by saving your airline discount site into this folder, you'll know exactly where to look for it next time. So click on the Travel folder to choose that as the location to save your site. Then, click the blue Add button to "bookmark" this site.

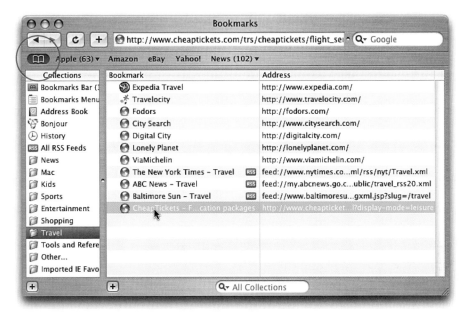

STEP EIGHTEEN (Finding Your Bookmarks):

When you later want to find a website that you've bookmarked (such as our airline discounts site), just click on the Bookmarks icon that appears near the top-left corner of the browser window (to the left of the word Apple) to reveal your collection of bookmarks. Then click on the Travel folder along the left side of the window and all the travel sites Apple already picked for you will be listed there, and at the bottom of the list will be your airline discount site. To visit that site, just double-click on it.

Turn on your AirPort Card

Choose a wireless network

STEP NINETEEN (Using Wireless Internet Access):
If you have a PowerBook or iBook, you're going to want to know how to jump on a Wireless network, since they're popping up everywhere, from McDonald's to Starbucks, from most every airport departure gate to Internet cafes. All you need is an Apple AirPort card. (*Note:* AirPort is Apple's name for their wireless Internet connection device. Your PowerBook or iBook may have come with an AirPort card built right in. To find out if yours has a built-in AirPort card, go under the Apple menu and choose About This Mac. When the About This Mac window appears, click on the More Info button. In a few seconds another window will appear with info about your particular Macintosh model. On the left side you'll see a list of contents. Look in the Network section, and if you see the words "AirPort Card," you're in luck. If it's not listed there, you don't have one, but you can buy one from Apple.com or your local Apple store in the mall.) To jump on a wireless network, first click on any empty space on your desktop (or click on the Finder icon in your Dock). Then, up in the menu bar at the top of your screen, you'll see a tiny icon that looks like a pie slice along the right side (it's supposed to be a radar icon, but face it—it's a pie slice). Click once on that icon, then with your mouse move down to Turn AirPort On and click on it once. If it finds a nearby wireless network, you'll see the pie slice fill with bands (now it looks more like radar), and if you click once on the radar (pie slice) icon, you'll see a list of the wireless networks it has found. To join one, just click on it, then launch the Safari Web browser, and you're on the Web.

6

Time

Goals

This lesson takes approximately 10 minutes to complete.

To learn how to set up different "widgets," so they'll automatically provide information you need from the Internet, along with other time-saving mini-applications to help you accomplish everyday tasks more efficiently.

Keeping in Touch with Your World Using Dashboard

The Internet is an amazing place for gathering information. It's especially useful for giving you instant access to commonly sought-after information, such as what the weather will be like today, how your stocks are doing right this minute, whether your flight's on time, and referencing online dictionaries and phonebooks. If you wind up doing at least some of these things every day (I know I do), you're going to spend a lot of your life staring at your Safari Web browser (the application we use on Macs to visit different websites). Well, rather than seeking out this information every day, and going to all these different websites, what if there was a way for this information to find you? For example, what if the weather report for your hometown was already waiting for you when you went to your Mac? And what if you also already had the weather for the cities your kids live in (providing, of course, that you have kids and they've moved out)? And what if your stock portfolio was already updated and all you had to do was glance at it? Wouldn't that be helpful? Too bad that kind of thing doesn't exist. Okay, I was baiting you. It does exist in Mac OS X Tiger's Dashboard. But Dashboard is more than just having your hand-picked Internet information waiting for you—it's also one-click access to other parts of your world, like your Address Book, calendars, a lightning-fast dictionary and thesaurus, and even iTunes. Best of all, these mini-applications (Apple calls them "widgets") are just one click away (or one keystroke away, depending on just how lazy you want to be).

STEP ONE (Getting to Your Dashboard):

There are two ways to get to Dashboard, and you can choose whichever one is easiest for you. You can get to Dashboard directly from the Dock at the bottom of your screen by clicking on the Dashboard icon (it looks similar to a gauge on a car's dashboard), or by pressing the F12 key on your keyboard (the Function keys are those keys that appear at the very top of your keyboard, and they start on the left with F1, F2, etc.).

QUITTING DASHBOARD

TIP ▶ If you want to close Dashboard at any time, either click on anything else outside of Dashboard (in the background of your desktop) or just press F12 again.

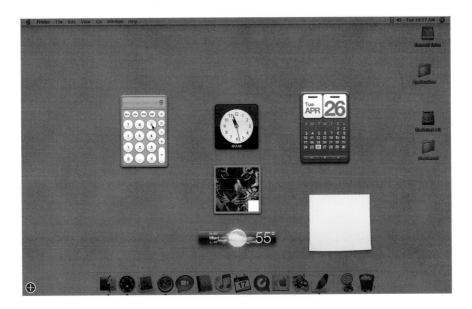

STEP TWO (Your First Look at Dashboard):

When you click on the Dashboard Dock icon (or press F12), Dashboard immediately zooms into view, with some of Dashboard's "widgets" (that's Apple's name for these mini-applications) already open (as shown above). We're going to start by looking at the Calculator widget on the left, which is probably the simplest of all widgets. It's pretty much just what it looks like—a calculator. It's handy for doing simple calculations, by either using the mouse and clicking on the calculator buttons, or you can use the numeric keypad on your keyboard (it's up to you). You can move the Calculator widget anywhere onscreen, so if you want it out of the way somewhere, click on any part of the calculator that isn't a button and drag it where you want it onscreen. Now, it will always appear in that spot (unless you decide to move it later). That's basically how you move widgets around—click on something other than their buttons, then drag them where you want them. So, if you want to take a moment to tidy up your widgets, I don't mind waiting.

STEP THREE (Closing Widgets You Don't Want):

Okay, let's say you don't want that Calculator widget to appear at all (after all, there is a more powerful calculator in your Applications folder if you really need to do some serious calculations). To close a widget, hold the Option key (it's along the bottom-left side of your keyboard), then move your mouse over the widget you want to close (in this case, the Calculator). As soon as your cursor moves over the Calculator, a little circle with an X on it will appear just outside the top-left corner of the widget. That's the Close button, so just move your mouse onto the Close button and click (while still pressing the Option key). That's it—you closed a widget.

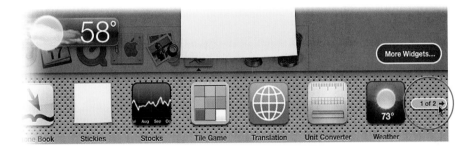

STEP FOUR (Getting More Widgets):

When you first open Dashboard, a few of the Dashboard widgets appear onscreen, but they're just a sample— actually there are more of them. To see the collection of widgets that come with Mac OS X Tiger, just click the little plus sign (+) button in the bottom-left corner of your screen (you'll only see this button when Dashboard is open) and a row of widgets (called the Widget Bar) will pop up across the bottom of your screen (well, they don't actually pop up; they kind of push everything else on your screen up an inch or two to temporarily make room for them). At least one long row of widgets will appear, and depending on the width of your Mac's monitor, there may be another row that's hidden off to the side. If that's the case, you'll see a right-facing arrow on the far-right side of the Widget Bar. Click on it, and the second row of widgets will appear (remember, you'll only see this second row if your monitor isn't wide enough to display them all at once, which is the case with most PowerBooks and iBooks).

CLOSING THE WIDGET BAR

TIP ▶ Once you open the Widget Bar, it stays open until you close it. You do that by clicking on the X button in the bottom left-hand corner of your screen (it's the same button you clicked to open the Widget Bar, but it changes to an X when you have the Widget Bar open).

STEP FIVE (Trying Out Widgets):

We've tried out one of the most basic widgets (the Calculator); now let's move onto something cooler. With the Widget Bar open, click once on the Unit Converter widget (it shows a ruler, a grid, and a gold bar stacked together) and it will appear onscreen. (When widgets appear, they arrive using a very slick little effect that kind of looks like a pond ripple.) The Unit Converter is one of those widgets that works fine for most things without being connected to the Internet (for example, it will convert miles per hour into kilometers per hour, gallons into liters, yards into meters, etc.). But if you're connected to the Internet, it can do some really handy stuff, so make sure you're connected to the Internet before we go any further.

In the top center of the Unit Converter widget is a pop-up menu to the right of the word "Convert" that lets you choose what you want to convert. Click once on this pop-up menu and choose Currency. As you know, currency prices fluctuate every day, but since you're connected to the Internet, when you ask it to convert dollars (by choosing US Dollar from the left pop-up menu) to Euros (by choosing Euro from the right pop-up menu), you're going to get an accurate conversion based on the latest currency rates. That's mighty cool stuff. This example gives you just a hint of how widgets can bring information from the Web right to your fingertips—without having to search for it using your Web browser.

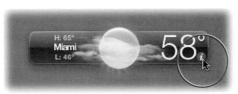

Default Weather widget

Choosing a new hometown for the Weather widget

STEP SIX (Setting Up Your Hometown Weather):
One of my favorite widgets is the Weather widget. It's one of the widgets already open when you first opened Dashboard (it looks like a dark blue vertical rectangle—well, it does now, anyway). For this Weather widget to give you the local forecast, you need to tell it where you live. You do this by clicking on the tiny, lowercase "i" icon that appears in the bottom right-hand corner when you move your mouse over the Weather widget. Click on that little "i" and your widget will "flip" around (like turning over a card), and on the back there's a text field where you enter your city, state, or ZIP code. Since we're setting this up for you, you probably know your own ZIP code (please tell me you know your own ZIP code), so click in the text field, enter your ZIP code, and then click the Done button in the bottom-right corner of the widget. (If you're connected to the Internet, your local forecast will immediately appear.) Best of all, your Weather widget will remember your ZIP code, so each day your weather forecast will be waiting for you.

TRACKING THE WEATHER IN OTHER CITIES

TIP If you want to track the weather in another city (perhaps you're traveling there soon, or you have friends or relatives there), just click on the plus sign (+) button in the bottom-left corner of your screen, then from the Widget Bar that appears, click on Weather. Type in the new city, and now it will be tracked each day for you along with your hometown Weather widget.

STEP SEVEN (Finding Even More Widgets):

Although Mac OS X Tiger comes with its own collection of widgets, you can download even more widgets for free, directly from Apple. All you have to do is click the plus sign (+) button in the left-hand corner of your screen (while Dashboard is open) to make the Widget Bar visible. Then, once the Widget Bar appears (or should I say "it moves into place"), look just above the bar on the far-right corner of your screen and you'll see a little button named More Widgets. Click once on that button. Your Web browser will launch (most likely Safari), and if you're connected to the Internet, it will take you directly to a special page on Apple's website where you'll find even more cool widgets that you can download. Once you download new widgets, they will appear in your Widget Bar when you relaunch Dashboard.

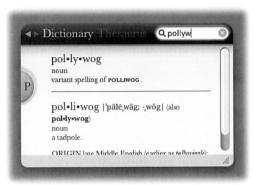

The Dictionary widget

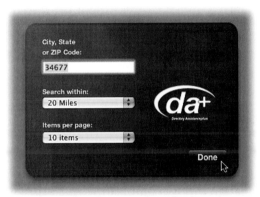

Editing the Phone Book widget's options

STEP EIGHT (Using Other Widgets):
Most of the widgets that come with Mac OS X Tiger are fairly easy to figure out on your own (like the Calculator, for example). The Dictionary widget is fairly easy to figure out too—just click on the Dictionary widget in the Widget Bar, then start typing the word you want to define and press the Return key. After you've searched for one word, it starts to work much like Mac OS X Tiger's Spotlight search, because as soon as you start typing again in the Search field, it starts looking for a match. By the time you get all (or most) of the word typed, the definition is already there waiting for you. If you want to switch to a thesaurus, just click once directly on the word "Thesaurus" that appears to the right of the word "Dictionary." The Phone Book widget works pretty much the same way as the Dictionary widget (and you open it from the Widget Bar as well). Take a few minutes to try out each widget in the Widget Bar.

*The iTunes and Flight Tracker widgets are just two of the many
widgets that you can customize by clicking on the "i" icon.*

STEP NINE (Tips for Widgets):
When you're trying out widgets, remember these three tips:

(1) There may be more to a widget than meets the eye (meaning, you can tweak
how it works or add some custom information to suit your needs) if you move
your cursor over the widget and a tiny "i" icon appears somewhere on the
widget. Click the "i" icon to access the options that will allow you to customize
the widget to your liking.

(2) Some widgets can't work properly unless your Mac is connected to the
Internet (like the one that tracks your stocks, for example), so make sure you're
online when you start trying these out.

(3) To close a widget, press-and-hold the Option key and then move your
cursor over the widget you want to close. When an X button appears in the
widget's top-left corner, click on it to close it.

7

Time

This lesson takes approximately 15 minutes to complete.

Goals

To set up your Mac to use text, audio, and even video chatting using Apple's iChat software, then to converse with friends and co-workers via the Internet using iChat.

How to Chat with Friends Online

Text chatting (the ability to have an online conversation by typing messages between computers) has been around for years now, and Mac OS X Tiger comes with one of the best-designed, best-implemented, and most fun interfaces for text chatting that's available today. But if you just text chat, you're missing one of the coolest experiences you can have on your Mac—video chatting. iChat AV lets you text chat, audio chat (which is kind of like an internet-based phone), and, of course, video chat. You only need two extra things to start video chatting: a video camera and a high-speed Internet connection. Apple makes a brilliant camera called iSight that's custom designed to work with iChat and your Mac. It's really an engineering marvel, in that it requires no configuration—you just plug it in, launch iChat, and it works. It's a beautiful thing. If you don't have an iSight camera (they're available at either Apple.com or your local Apple Store), you can even hook up your own personal digital video camcorder and use it instead (but trust me, if you're going to be doing a reasonable amount of video chatting, you'll want an iSight camera). In this chapter, you're going to learn how to text chat, audio chat, and video chat, all using the slickest chatting software available anywhere. Best of all, it comes free with Mac OS X Tiger.

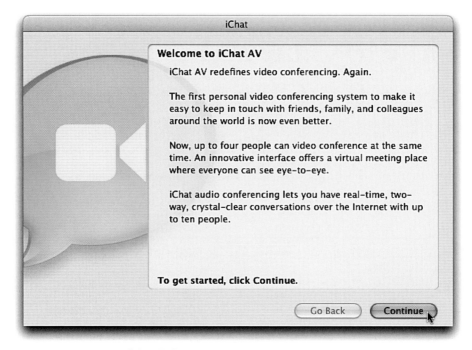

STEP ONE (Launching iChat):

To start chatting with your friends, your first step is to launch iChat by clicking on the iChat icon in the Dock at the bottom of your screen (its icon looks like a blue cartoon conversation bubble with a white movie camera icon in the middle). The first time you launch iChat, a window will appear to help you configure it. When it appears, click the Continue button.

STEP TWO (Creating Accounts So You Can Chat):

To use iChat, you will need either an America Online Instant Messenger account (called an AIM account, which is an acronym for AOL Instant Messenger) or a .Mac account with Apple (which I strongly urge you to sign up for, but email and chatting is just a small part of why you should have a .Mac account—more on this later). If you have a .Mac account, you can enter your Account Name and Password in the fields provided. If you don't have a .Mac account yet, you can get an iChat account and a 60-day free .Mac trial by clicking on the Get an iChat Account button that appears just below the Password field in the iChat setup window. This takes you to a website where you can sign up for the free trial (it also tells you some of the benefits of getting a .Mac account, so take a minute or two to check it out). Otherwise, you can create an AIM account (by visiting www.aim.com and downloading the AIM software). The website will have an online form in which you create an AIM account (and it's free).

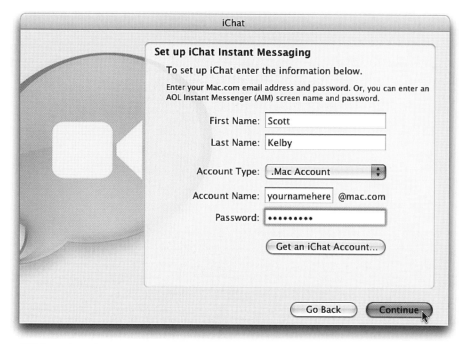

STEP THREE (Preparing iChat):

Once you sign up and get a screen name and password (be it .Mac or AIM), enter that info into the iChat setup window. Then, click the blue Continue button. In fact, keep hitting the Continue button until it turns into the Done button. Once it shows the Done button, click it—it's time to chat!

STEP FOUR (Asking for Your Friends' Screen Names):

Alright, now that you've configured your iChat, the Buddy List window will appear onscreen. This is where you put the screen names of your friends and co-workers who either have .Mac or AIM accounts. So how do you find your friends' screen names? It's simple. You ask them. Drop them an email, mention that you want to add them to your Buddy List, and if they like you, there's a reasonable chance they'll give you their screen names. Once you have those, you'll want to enter them into your Buddy List, so anytime they're online and available for a chat, you'll be able to simply double-click on their name in your iChat Buddy List and invite them to chat. You enter their screen name by going under iChat's Buddies menu (at the very top of your screen) and choosing Add Buddy (or click on the plus sign [+] button in the bottom-left corner of the Buddy List window).

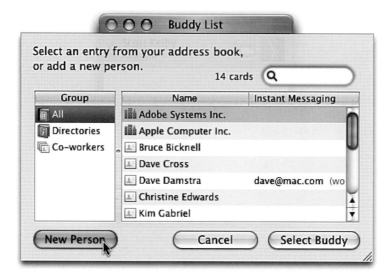

STEP FIVE (Searching for Friends' Screen Names):

If you have their information already entered in your Address Book (including their screen name), you can just enter their name the Search field in the top-right corner of the window to find their screen name and iChat will do the rest. However, if you haven't had a chance to enter their screen name into your Address Book yet, just click on the New Person button in the bottom-left corner of the window.

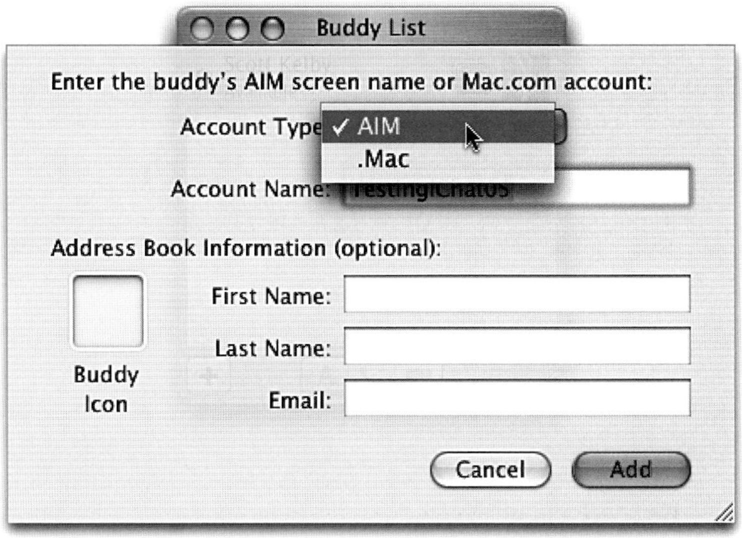

STEP SIX (Adding Screen Names):

A new window will pop down in which you can choose the type of account the person has (either .Mac or AIM), and then their Account Name (screen name). If you want, you can enter a first and last name and email address, which will then be added to your Address Book, but adding them is optional. Once the info is entered, click the Add button, and you have your first buddy.

STEP SEVEN (Seeing Who Is Available to Chat):

Once you've entered one or more friends to your Buddy List, their screen names will appear in the Buddy List window. If they're offline, their names will be "grayed out," and double-clicking on them won't do anything because they're not online—you can only chat with people who are both online *and* have iChat open. However, if they're available online, their name will appear in black. If they're available to chat now, you'll see a green dot appear before their name. If you see a red dot before their name, it means that they're online, they have iChat open, but for some reason they're not available to chat right now (maybe they've stepped away from their computer, they're on a phone call, etc.). If you see a yellow dot before their name, that shows their computer is idle, meaning they haven't used their computer for a while, so there's a good chance they stepped away from their computer while still logged into iChat. Glancing at these colored buttons instantly lets you know whether the person you're about to contact is available for chat.

MAKING YOURSELF UNAVAILABLE FOR CHATTING

TIP ▶ By the way, if you want to change your status from "available" to "away," look in the top-left corner of the Buddy List window, directly beneath where your name appears. Just click once on the word "Available" and a list of choices will pop up. If you don't want to use Away, choose Custom. You can now type any message you want your buddies to see. (Maybe something like "I'm on the phone—be right back!" or "Went for coffee, back in two minutes," etc.) So now that you know how to check someone's chat availability, in the next step we'll invite someone to chat.

STEP EIGHT (Inviting Someone to Chat):

So let's say you see a buddy is online (their name appears in black and they're available to chat now because there's a green button before their name). If you want to invite them to a text chat, just double-click on their name and a chat window will open. You'll see the icon representing you (hopefully it's not a soccer ball) in the top of the window and at the bottom is a text field where you type your invitation. You can type in anything you like here (it can be as simple as "Hi!"). Once you're done typing, press the Return key and you'll see your "Hi!" appear in a conversation bubble beside your name and image icon.

STEP NINE (What Your Buddy Sees):
At the same time, a tiny window will pop up on your buddy's screen indicating there's a chat message waiting. (For example, if I were inviting you to a chat, it would say "Chat with Scott Kelby.") When your buddy clicks anywhere on the window (that is, if they're using iChat too), it expands into an instant chat window with buttons from which your buddy can choose: (1) Decline: This simply makes your message disappear from their screen without any explanation required, meaning they simply aren't going to respond to you. (2) Block: They'll only choose this if they're mad at you, because this blocks you from ever inviting them to chat again. This was designed for iStalkers. (3) Accept: If your buddy chooses to accept your invitation, they can type something in their text field, press the Return key, and reply back to you (and you'll see their responses on the left side of your chat window).

STEP TEN (Ending Your Chat):

Once your buddy responds, the chat is on—so start typin'! To end your chat, first be sure to tell the person goodbye (hey, it's only polite), then click on the red button in the top-left corner of your chat window. This closes the window and ends your chat.

STEP ELEVEN (Adding Your Photo Icon):

When you talk in a text chat, you're likely represented by either a blue globe icon or a soccer ball icon by default. That's great if you indeed look like a soccer ball or a blue globe, but the whole experience will feel much more natural (and more conversational) if you use your photo instead, rather than Apple's blue globe icon, which is kind of worldly, yet somewhat impersonal. First, you'll need to import a photo of yourself (preferably a head shot) into your Mac (you can go to Lesson 4 "Importing Photos" if you don't know how). Your photo will wind up in the Pictures folder on your hard disk, so open that folder, find your head shot, click-and-hold on it, then drag-and-drop it onto the blue globe (or ball) icon in iChat.

STEP TWELVE (Adjusting Your Photo Icon):

Once you drag-and-drop your picture on the iChat icon, the Buddy Picture editing window will appear. The clear rectangle in the middle of the dialog shows what area of your photo will appear—the shaded areas will be cropped away. To reposition your photo so it better fits in that clear rectangle, you can click-and-hold directly on your photo, then drag your photo around to where you want it. You can also change the size of your photo by dragging the slider directly under the photo editing area. When the position and sizing look good to you, click the Set button (in the bottom right of the window), and you're set (sorry, that was lame).

USING ISIGHT TO SNAP A SHOT

TIP If you don't have a head shot, but you do have an Apple iSight camera connected to your Mac (used for video chats), you can use that video camera to take your photo. Just go under the Buddies menu and choose Change My Picture and the Edit window will open. Then click on the Take Video Snapshot button. In a few seconds, iSight will snap a picture of you, and then you can edit that picture in the Buddy Picture editing window.

STEP THIRTEEN (Audio Chats):

If both you and the person you want to chat with have built-in microphones (you both have a PowerBook, iBook, iMac, or eMac), you can choose to audio chat. If they're available for an audio chat, a green telephone icon will appear to the immediate left of their photo (or globe icon, etc.) on the right side of the Buddy List window. To invite them to an audio chat, just click directly on that green telephone button, and a little audio chat invitation window will appear on your buddy's screen, with an audible ringing sound (kind of like a phone). It will continue to ring until your buddy clicks on the window. At that point, your buddy has the same answering options as with a text chat: They can Decline (in which case, you'll see the message "Your Buddy has declined your invitation," which will usually initiate a call to your therapist); they can send a Text Reply (in case they're on the phone); or they can Accept, in which case it will take just a few seconds to connect, then you can start talking. *Note:* To quit the audio chat, click the small red button in the top left-hand corner of the window.

STEP FOURTEEN (Muting Your Audio Chat):

If you need to mute your audio (you need to sneeze or make other unpleasant audible sounds), click on the Mute button (it looks like a microphone with a line through it) in the audio chat window. The green voice level meter will turn orange to let you know you're muted. To resume speaking, click the Mute button again. If you want to add other people to your audio chat (you want an audio conference), just click on the plus sign (+) button to the left of the Mute button, and you can then invite additional buddies to the audio chat.

STEP FIFTEEN (Preparing for a Video Chat):

If you have one of Apple's iSight cameras, you can use iChat to do live real-time video chats. (If you don't have an Apple iSight, you can buy one at Apple.com or your local Apple Store. I have to say, they're brilliantly designed and require no configuration at all—you just plug them into the FireWire port on your Mac and they work—first time!) Okay, so basically the first part is doing just that—plugging the FireWire cable that comes with your iSight camera into the FireWire port on your Mac. Then, place the camera on the top of your monitor (a mounting bracket comes with the camera) and launch iChat. You'll see a little green camera button appear to the left of your photo (or icon) in the top-right corner of the iChat window, which lets you know your camera is hooked up and ready to go (also, now your buddies will see that your camera is hooked up and ready to go).

STEP SIXTEEN (Inviting a Buddy to a Video Chat):

To invite one of your buddies to a video chat, all you need to do is click on the green camera icon that appears to the left of their photo in the Buddy List window (if you don't see a camera icon to the right of their screen name next to their icon, they don't have their camera hooked up). When you do this, a new window appears, and it shows a preview of the view from your camera, so you can reposition it, comb your hair, etc., and while it's previewing, it's contacting your buddy. If your buddy accepts your invitation, they will appear full size in your preview window, and your preview image will shrink down to the right-hand corner (kind of like picture-in-picture on a TV set). That's it—you're video chatting.

STEP SEVENTEEN (Video Chatting with More Than One Person):
If you've got a pretty fast Mac (like a Dual 1-GHz G4 or any G5), you can
have a video conference with up to three of your buddies (provided, of
course, they all have iSight cameras connected to their computers). Here's
how it works: Just click on the first person you want in your video conference,
then hold the Command key on your keyboard (that's the one with the Apple
logo on it, just to the left of the Spacebar on your keyboard) and click on the
other people in your Buddy List that you want in your video conference to
select them. Now, click on the Start a Video Chat button (it looks like a video
camera) at the bottom of your Buddy List window to invite them to your video
conference. The ones that accept will join in and will be displayed in separate
windows within the iChat window. To end your video chat, wave goodbye
(just kidding), then click the red button in the upper left-hand corner of
your iChat camera window.

8

Time

Goals

This lesson takes approximately 10 minutes to complete.

To learn how to locate different types of documents on your Mac, including photos, movies, text documents, and more, using Mac OS X Tiger's Spotlight search feature.

Finding Things on Your Mac

Okay, you're downloading songs, you're creating text documents, you're downloading and importing movie clips, you're doing all kinds of cool stuff, and all the while you're saving these documents in different places on your Mac. Saving stuff is easy. Finding the exact file you want three weeks later has been kind of tough over the years. In fact, although Apple called the feature "Find," it was really more like "Scour," because you spent a lot of time searching before you could actually find the file you wanted. But Mac OS X Tiger changes all of that with a new feature called Spotlight. I have to say Spotlight is somewhat of a mini-miracle unto itself. What makes it so amazing—besides the sheer lightning-fast speed with which it finds files—is that it's designed to help you find files that you don't actually know the exact name of. In fact, if you even have a close stab at what the file name could be or can even remember a word that might be in the document (or if you can't remember either of those things, just that you created the file about a week ago), Spotlight will not only find it for you in seconds, it will actually launch the application you created the file with. Then, it will open the document so you can see if it's the right one. And it does all of this with incredible ease and speed. It actually takes the act of finding files and transforms it from a frustrating, time-intensive task into a quick, fun experience. It's hard to think of a search feature that's cool enough to actually make you smile the first time you use it, but I'll bet you this—Spotlight will do just that. It's one of those things that makes you nod your head and say, "Isn't technology amazing?"

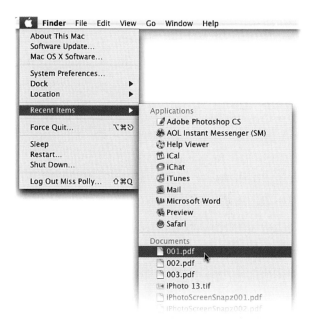

STEP ONE (Where to Look First):

Okay, so you've been working on your Mac for a while—you've been downloading songs, importing photos, creating text documents, sending and receiving emails, etc.—and so far everything has basically been one big love fest. But at some point, you're going to say to yourself, "Hey, where did I save that file with my ideas for next summer's family reunion?" If you saved it fairly recently (maybe earlier today or within the last day or so), you might be able to get right to it. Start by clicking once on the Apple menu (found in the upper-left corner of your screen), and then with your cursor arrow, move down to Recent Items and a flyout menu will appear. Your most recently used applications are at the top of the list, but directly below that (in the Documents section) are the last 10 documents you opened. If the one you're looking for is in that menu, just slide your mouse over, move down to that document, click the mouse once on it in the list, and the document will open. Hey, it's worth a try.

STEP TWO (Where to Look Next: Spotlight):
So what if the file you saved a couple of days ago (let's say it was a list of people you're inviting to your next party) wasn't in that Recent Items menu? Now what do you do? You reach for Spotlight (Mac OS X Tiger's built-in search feature). Luckily, you don't have to go far, because no matter what you're doing (or which application you're working in), you can always access Spotlight. It's located at the top-right corner of your screen (its icon is a blue circle with a magnifying glass in it). When you want to search for something, click once on that icon, and the Spotlight Search field will appear.

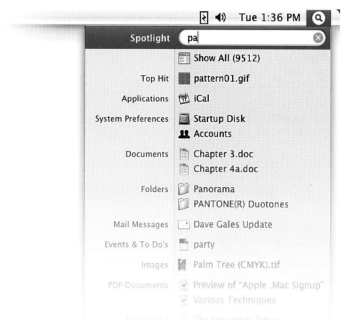

STEP THREE (Using Spotlight):

Now that you know where Spotlight lives (in the upper right-hand corner of your screen), let's give it a whirl. Click on the blue Spotlight icon and the Spotlight Search field will pop down. If you were looking for that party invitation list you created a few days ago (let's say you named that file "Party People" or "Party List" or "Invite List"), you'd just start typing in the word "party," and as soon as you type just the "pa" in "party," Spotlight starts bringing up results. It's amazingly fast and complete; it instantly displays everything on your computer that contains the word "party." Not just files named "party"—we're talking everything. It searches your email (both your email inbox and emails you've sent), it searches your Address Book, it searches your iCal calendars—everything—and displays it in a window just below the Search field.

ERASING YOUR LAST SEARCH

TIP ▶ Let's say you searched for the word "party" earlier, and now you want to search for the word "Apple." The word "party" will still appear in the Spotlight Search field, but you can instantly clear it by clicking on the little X on the far-right side of the Search field.

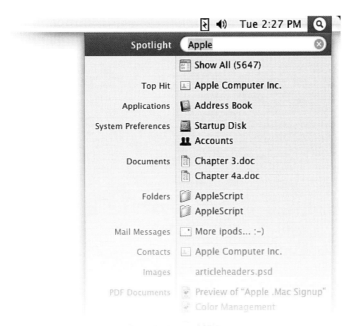

STEP FOUR (Working with the Results):

The files Spotlight finds are listed in order by what it thinks you're most likely looking for. How does it know? Well, if it finds a file with the exact word or phrase you entered, it puts that file at the top of the list. So, for example, let's do a Spotlight search for Apple Computer's customer service number. You know you have their phone number somewhere on your Mac, but you can't quite remember where (just so you know, Apple puts their customer service number in your Address Book by default, but let's pretend I didn't just tell you that). To find that information, you'd go to Spotlight and type "Apple" in the Search field. When the results appear, you'll see that Apple Computer winds up at the top of the list in the Top Hit section. It figures that's probably what you were looking for.

NARROWING YOUR SEARCH

TIP ▶ Although Spotlight starts searching the moment you type a letter, the more letters you type, the more focused your results will be. For example, if you type the word "North," you might get dozens of results; but if you type "Northern," Spotlight will narrow your search. If you type "Northern Region," it will narrow the search even further to only files that have the words "Northern Region" in them.

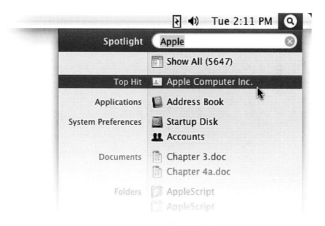

STEP FIVE (Seeing Instant Results):
Although Spotlight will easily identify hundreds of different files on your
Mac that contain the word "Apple," it thankfully only displays the most likely
matches in the results list. Because it separates them by type of document, it
helps you quickly see if a particular file is the one you want. (For example,
if one of the results came from your iCal calendar, and you're looking for a
phone number, you can probably ignore the calendar result.) Now, let's look at
that Top Hit—it shows Apple Computer, right? But we're not 100% sure that's
the file we want until we open it, so just click directly on that result in the
list, and Spotlight will actually launch the Address Book application, opening
it to the contact page for Apple Computer (where you'll find Apple's phone
number). How slick is that? So that's how it works—when you find a result that
you think is the file you're looking for, click on it, and in just a few seconds,
you'll know for sure because it will open for you.

STEP SIX (Seeing More Results):

Now, although the results list only displays the top two matches in each category for your search of the word "Apple," how many total results did Spotlight find? It displays that number at the top of the list (on my iMac, it came up with 5,647 total results). To see all the results, move your mouse cursor over Show All at the top and click. Spotlight will open in its own separate window, displaying all 5,647 results sorted by category (well, it shows the top five results in each category. If you *really* want to see all the results in each category, after the five that are listed, you'll see a line that reads something like "225 more..." or "48 more..." or however many files are left to view. Click directly on that line of text and you'll see the rest). If you double-click on any of the results in this window, that file will open. If Spotlight has to launch an application for you to see the file—don't worry—it'll do it for you. It's like a file-finding concierge.

SPOTLIGHT IS BUILT INTO SOME APPLICATIONS

TIP ▸ There are certain Mac OS X Tiger applications that have built-in Spotlight searching (in other words, it gives the same lightning-fast, super-complete results, but just for what it finds in that application). These include Mail, iCal, and Address Book, so you'll see the familiar-looking Search field in the interface of each.

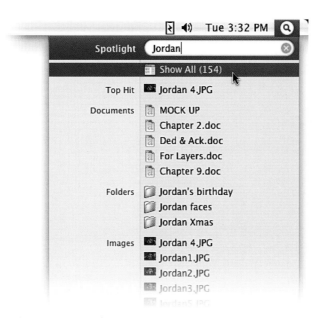

STEP SEVEN (Finding the Right Photo, Part 1):
Spotlight does its finest work when you're searching for things like photos, movies, and music. For example, let's say you want to find a particular photo you took at your kid's birthday party. You're not sure of the photo's exact file name, but you do remember you named those photos with your kid's name ("Jordan" in this case). Well, here's where Spotlight pitches in to help. Start by going to the Spotlight Search field and typing "Jordan." Instantly, the results list will appear, and you'll see your Top Hit at the top of the list. Below that you'll see all the images that have the name "Jordan" in their file name. So how can you tell which photo is the right one? Go on to the next step.

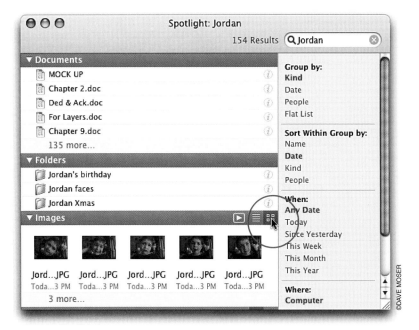

STEP EIGHT (Finding the Right Photo, Part 2):

Well, here's where it gets fun. Click on the Show All button at the top of the results list, so Spotlight opens in its own separate window. You see how your photos (under the Images section) are shown as tiny thumbnail icons? I know—they're too small to discern which photo is the one you're looking for. Well, there are two ways Spotlight can help: (1) In the blue Images section divider, click directly on the little four-square button on the right (it's circled above), and your photos will be displayed with much larger icons so you can see which one is which. If that's still not big enough for ya, (2) click on the Play button on the right in the blue Images section divider and all those photos will be displayed one-by-one in a full-screen slide show. When you see the one you want, just press the Escape (Esc) key on your keyboard to stop the slide show. You can now access that photo by double-clicking directly on its icon. I told you this was gonna be fun. But we're not done yet….

STEP NINE (Finding Movies and Music):

If you're searching for QuickTime movies that you've downloaded from the Web or music files that you've imported or downloaded, Spotlight makes finding the right one easy by giving you previews from right within the main results window. For example, let's say you're searching for a song by The Beatles, but you're not sure of the song's name. Just type "Beatles," and when the results list appears, click on Show All. Once Spotlight opens in a separate window, you'll see all of your Beatles songs listed under the Music section. To hear one of the songs, click on it to select it, then to the far right of that song's listing, you'll see a tiny info button (it's a circle with a lowercase "i"). Click on that button, and Spotlight will instantly display all the info on that song. But there's more….

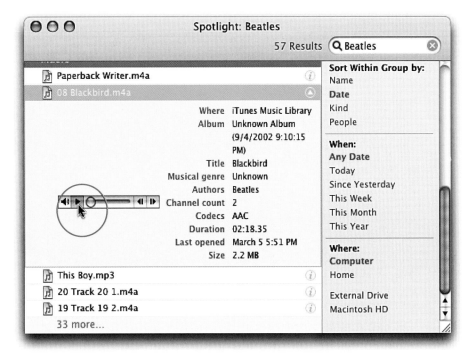

STEP TEN (Playing Music or Movies within Spotlight):

It gets better. There's a built-in music player so you can hear the song right within Spotlight. The music player appears as a thin, horizontal, silver-and-black bar to the left of the song's info (after you've clicked on the tiny info button). In the music player on the left side, you'll see a small right-facing arrow, which is the Play button. Click on it and your music will start playing. (*Note:* If for some reason you don't hear the music, make sure your Mac's volume is turned up by going to the top-right side of your Mac's screen and clicking once on the little speaker icon. A volume slider will appear. To increase the volume, click-and-hold on the little slider button and drag upward. When you release your mouse button, the little slider goes away. There's also a volume slider in the Spotlight music player—just click-and-hold on the little speaker icon in the left of the music player and a slider will appear.) So that's how you preview music. Movies work pretty much the same way—if you see a movie result and want to see a quick clip of it (to see if it's the one you're searching for), you'll do the same thing you did for music—click on a movie, click the little "i" button, then click the Play button in the movie player that appears. (*Note:* To stop either a movie or a song from playing, click on the Pause button, which had been the Play button.)

STEP ELEVEN (Sorting Your Results):

Alright, by now you're getting pretty good at searching. You know how to use the results to find just what you're looking for (thanks to them being categorized and with help from the photo, movie, and audio previews), and you even know how to open the documents Spotlight finds. But did you know that you can tweak how the results are displayed to make finding things easier for *you*, based on what *you're* looking for, and how *you* think? For example, let's look at the main Spotlight window (the separate window you get when you click on Show All). By default, all the results are grouped by the kind of document they are (so all the email results appear grouped in one section, all the photos in another, etc.). In the top-right corner of the Spotlight window (just under the Search field), there's a list named "Group By," and you can see the word "Kind" is blue. If you're not exactly sure of the name of the file, but you think you remember when you created it, try grouping by Date, or go down a little further on the right side of Spotlight and try some of the choices under When. If you know approximately when you created the file, it can really help you zero-in on where that file is, even if you don't know the full name of the file. For example, let's say you created a file earlier this month, and you think part of the name might include the word "vacation." Just search for the word "vacation," and when the results appear in the main Spotlight window, go to the When list on the right side and click on This Month. Now only the documents you created this month will be visible, helping you narrow the search even more. This is pretty handy stuff.

9

This lesson takes approximately 10 minutes to complete.

To set up a system for saving your work so you'll not only be able to find your saved files with ease, but also protect your work from accidental loss.

How to Save Your Work So You Can Use It Again Later

So far, the applications we've been using all automatically save the changes you've made since the last time you opened the application. For example, if you imported songs from a music CD into iTunes, those songs are still there the next time you open iTunes, right? Right. Same thing with iCal—it saves all your appointments when you quit iCal. Even if you don't open iCal again for weeks, all your stuff is still there. However, most other applications will require you to save your work before you're done. (For example, remember that fictitious list of people you were going to invite to your next party? Well, once you created your list, you'd have to give it a name and save it.) But there's a little more to saving files than just clicking the Save button, because you have a decision to make: where to save the files on your hard disk. I know what you're thinking: "Since Mac OS X Tiger has Spotlight, why do I even care?" (You were thinking that, weren't you?) Well, here's the thing: Spotlight is great if you can't remember where you saved your files, but if you plan ahead and save your files in an easy-to-find place on your hard disk, then you won't even need Spotlight—you'll be able to go directly to your files. In fact, you'll only need Spotlight when you can't remember where you saved a file. In this lesson, we'll look at how and when to save your files, where to save them, and how to keep your hard disk neat and tidy so everything is right at your fingertips.

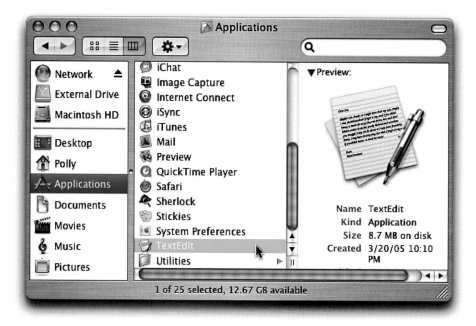

STEP ONE (Launching TextEdit):

Until now, we've just been using applications that already appear in the Dock at the bottom of your screen (or launch automatically like iPhoto), but Mac OS X Tiger ships with a number of other applications as well (they're all found in your Applications folder, which we'll get to in a moment). To learn how to create and save documents on your own, we're going to use an application called TextEdit, which is a very, very simple word processor (you can use it for basic letter writing, note taking, etc.). TextEdit is found in your Applications folder, and the quickest way to get there is to first click on the Finder icon in the Dock at the bottom of your screen (which should bring up a window onscreen). Then, press-and-hold these three keys on your keyboard at the same time: Shift-Command-A (just in case you missed it earlier, the Command key is the one with the Apple logo on it). This reveals all your installed applications in the window onscreen. By default, they're listed in alphabetical order, so if you don't see TextEdit right off the bat, it's probably because you have to scroll down the window to see it. Using your mouse, click-and-hold on the blue gel-like button on the right side of the window and drag it downward so you can see the other applications in this window. Keep dragging until you see TextEdit (if you pass it, drag that blue button upward again). Once you find it (its icon looks like a piece of paper with a pen resting on it), double-click on it to launch TextEdit.

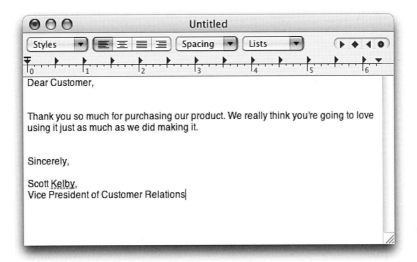

STEP TWO (Creating Your First Document—a Letter):
When TextEdit appears (it opens in about two seconds, which is one reason I love TextEdit), it opens a brand new blank document, ready for you to start typing (that's what that blinking thin black line is telling you—it's ready for you to start typing). For the sake of our example, we (and by we, I mean you) are going to create a simple business letter using TextEdit, so start typing the standard ol' "Dear Customer," salutation, then press the Return key on your keyboard three times (to move down a few lines). Type some friendly text (if you can't think of what to write, try this: "Thank you so much for purchasing our product. We really think you're going to love using it just as much as we did making it."). Press the Return key three more times and type "Sincerely," then press Return two more times and type your name. Press Return just once, and then type your title (which is "Vice President of Customer Relations" by the way—congratulations on having such a cool job). Okay, that's it. You've created your first document.

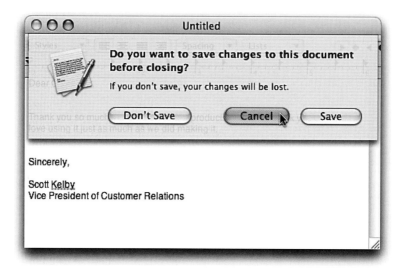

STEP THREE (To Save or Not to Save?):

It's decision time: You've created this letter and now you have to decide if this is a letter you want to save or not. If you decide that you don't want to save the letter, then take your mouse and click on the little round red button that appears in the upper-left corner of your TextEdit document (that's the Close button). Once you click the Close button, a little window will pop down with three choices on it (as shown above). If you didn't want to save this document, you'd click once on the Don't Save button on the left (don't actually click on it, I'm just telling you what to do if you didn't want to save your letter, but in this case, we do, so don't click any buttons yet). If indeed you had clicked the Don't Save button, the document would immediately close—it would not be saved anywhere, and it would just vanish as if it had never existed at all. So again, *don't* click the Don't Save button unless you really intend to never see that document again. Instead, click on the Cancel button in the window.

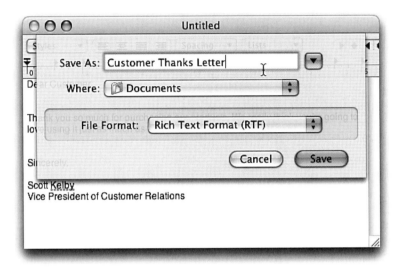

STEP FOUR (Naming Your File Before You Save It):

Okay, now we have the other decision: to save the letter (so you can open it again at a later time, maybe to make changes, print it out, etc.). We use a slightly different method when saving files (even though technically we could use that "click-the-Close-button" technique we learned in the previous step, because the window that pops down contains a Save button, but that method requires more steps). To save your letter, press-and-hold the Command key on your keyboard, and then press the S key (that's the shortcut for Save: Command-S). A little window will pop down from the top of your TextEdit letter. The first thing it wants you to do is give this file (your letter) a name in the Save As field (it's already highlighted the default name in the field, so all you have to do is start typing). I strongly recommend giving your letter a brief, yet descriptive name so it's easier to find later when you're looking for it. An example of a good name might be something like "Customer Thanks Letter," so go ahead and type that for the sake of our example. Of course, you can choose any name you like when you're working on your own files, but you'll find that the more descriptive the name, the easier your life will be down the road. You can type up to 256 characters if absolutely necessary, but brief, simple names are easier to remember (don't click Save yet).

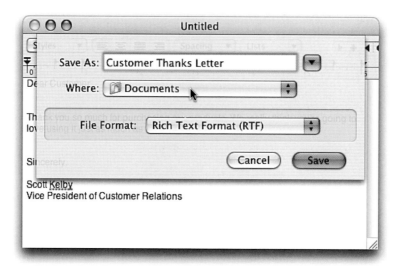

STEP FIVE (Where to Save Your File):

Apple has done something (on your behalf) to help you quickly find the files
you create. If you look in that Save window (see the previous step), you'll see
the word "Where" with a pop-up menu next to it. By default, Apple saves all the
documents you create in a folder called "Documents." This folder is similar to
one you'd use in a traditional filing cabinet. For example, in a traditional filing
cabinet, you don't just open the drawer, drop another sheet in, and close the
drawer, right? Instead you sort everything into separate, named folders. Well,
your Mac works the same way. It puts all your documents into a folder named
"Documents." That way, when you ask yourself the question, "Where did I save
that letter?" you'll know that it was saved in your Documents folder (we'll look
at how to find things in your Documents folder in a few moments). So, basically,
this Documents folder is where you want to save documents. Apple has created
other folders for saving other sorts of files. For example, there's a Pictures folder
for saving your photos, a Music folder for saving music, and a Movies folder
for saving movies. *Note:* I wasn't going to mention this (because doing what I'm
about to tell you may cause utter chaos), but if you don't want to save your file in
the Documents folder, you can choose a different folder from the Where pop-up
menu. Now forget I told you that, as your life will be so much simpler if you
keep your documents in the Documents folder. *Another note:* If you want to see
exactly where the file is being saved on your hard disk, click on the down-facing
arrow to the far right of the Save As field. This will show you a folder-by-folder
breakdown of your hard disk.

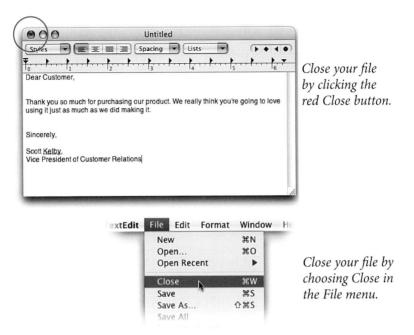

Close your file
by clicking the
red Close button.

Close your file by
choosing Close in
the File menu.

STEP SIX (Actually Saving Your File):

Ah, the time has come at last to save your letter. By now you've named it and you
know it's going to be saved into the Documents folder, so all that's left to do is
click on the blue Save button. When you do this, your document will still remain
open, but the name you just gave your letter will appear at the top center of the
document's window. With your letter safely saved, you can either click the tiny
red Close button in the top-left corner of the TextEdit window or you can click
on the word "File" (at the top of your screen in the menu bar) and with your
mouse move down the menu to the word "Close," then click once.

SAVE OFTEN...OR ELSE...

TIP ▶ Let's say you're writing a chapter for a book. You wrote for an
hour or so, and then you saved the document. The next day, you open
that same document and start writing again. You've written for about
30 minutes, then suddenly the electricity goes out for just a minute or so.
When it comes back on, you restart your Mac, and then reopen the chapter
you were working on. Everything you wrote in the last 30 minutes will be
gone. That's because the last time you "saved" was yesterday. This is why
we save often while we're working (using that same Command-S keyboard
shortcut I showed you earlier).

STEP SEVEN (Finding the Documents Folder):
Okay, you saved and closed your letter. Now, how do you get it back? Since it's a document, you know to look in your Documents folder. To get to it, take your mouse and click once on any empty desktop space to activate the Finder application, then press-and-hold these three keys: Shift-Command-H. Your Home window will appear onscreen (this is kind of your home base, where you'll have access to all your *stuff*). In this window you'll see the Documents folder. To look inside that folder, just double-click directly on its icon, and all the documents you've saved (including your letter) will be there (much like if you went to a traditional filing cabinet in your office, pulled out the drawer, and pulled out a folder named "Documents"). Depending on how many documents you have in your folder, you may have to do some scrolling (up or down by dragging the blue gel-like button on the far-right side of the window), but if this letter is the first thing you've saved, you won't have much trouble finding it. To open it, just double-click on the document's icon, then TextEdit will launch and your document will open. Okay, so what happens when you do start saving a lot of files? You're about to find out.

CHANGING THE VIEW OF A WINDOW

TIP ▶ By default, your windows show all your documents as large icons. However, if you'd like to see the contents of your window as an alphabetical list, just click  on the List View button (nested in the group of three icons) in the top left of your window (its icon looks like four horizontal lines).

STEP EIGHT (Organizing Your Documents Folder):

Let's say that business is great, and you wind up writing quite a few letters. Before you know it, you've got dozens of letters in your Documents folder, along with dozens of other documents. The way to keep them organized is by (are you ready for this?) creating folders that live inside your Documents folder. Don't let this throw you, because just like a traditional filing cabinet, you'd have more than one folder in there, right? And there are probably some really thick folders in there that have some other folders inside, right? Well, that's all you're doing here (if you do this once, it will make more sense). So, let's create a folder called "Customer Thank-You Letters," into which we'll drag all those thank-you letters that are cluttering up your Documents folder. Now, you already have your Documents window open (from the previous step) so just take your mouse and click directly on the word "File" at the top left of your screen, and when the menu appears, move your mouse down to New Folder and click once. A new folder will appear in your Documents window and its name "untitled folder" will already be highlighted. All you have to do is type a new name, "Customer Thank-You Letters," and then press the Return key on your keyboard. Now, any customer service letters you see loose in the Documents folder need to go in this new folder, so click-and-hold on a letter's icon, drag it onto your new folder (when your letter moves over the folder, the folder will highlight), and release the mouse button to drop it right in.

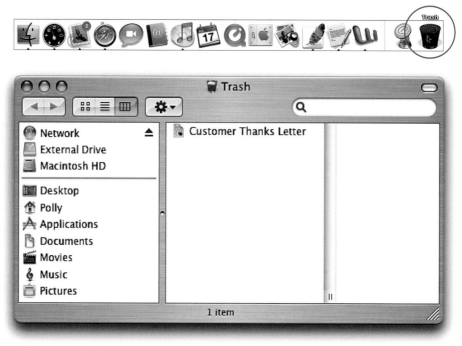

STEP NINE (Deleting Files):

So far, we've only been concerned with saving your documents, but what if you want to delete a document from your Mac? Just look in your Documents folder for the document you want to delete, then click-and-hold directly on that document's icon and drag it into the Trash icon that appears on the far-right side of the Dock at the bottom of your screen. Think of the Trash icon on your Mac much like a trash can in your kitchen. You put things in there, but they're not really "gone" until you take that can to the street and it's picked up by the local sanitation company. Anytime until that point, you can just reach into the garbage can in your kitchen and pull something out (like a half-eaten éclair). Your Mac's Trash is pretty much like that. You put things in there that you want thrown away, but they're not really gone until you choose Empty Trash (which is your Mac's equivalent of the sanitation truck pulling up and emptying the garbage [you'll learn how to empty the Trash in the next step]). Before you choose Empty Trash, just like in your kitchen, you can pull something back out of your Mac's Trash. You do that by clicking once on the Trash icon in the Dock. The Trash's window will appear onscreen, showing you all the stuff you've put in there (that's right—*stuff*). If you see a document you wish you hadn't trashed, just click-and-drag it out of the Trash onto your Mac's desktop. If you wipe it clean with a moist towel, you can still probably eat it (okay, that was really lame—sorry).

STEP TEN (Deleting Files for Good by Emptying the Trash):
Once something is in your Trash, you can empty the Trash by first clicking anywhere on your empty desktop to make the Finder application active. Then, click once on the word "Finder" in the menu bar at the top of your screen. When the menu appears, move your mouse down to Empty Trash and click on it once. You'll get a warning dialog that asks: "Are you sure you want to remove the items in the Trash permanently?" If you click the OK button, they're gone for good, so make sure that's what you really want to do.

10

Time

Goals

This lesson takes approximately 10 minutes to complete.

To learn strategies for maximizing your PowerBook's or iBook's battery life.

Lesson **10**

Using Your PowerBook or iBook Portable

When it comes to Mac OS X Tiger, it really doesn't matter which type of Mac you run it on (iMac, G5, Mac mini, etc.) because it's pretty much a consistent experience, and that's a good thing. However, if you have a PowerBook or an iBook (Apple's versions of the "laptop" computer), you'll want to become a master of battery management, and you'll be exploring a few areas of Mac OS X Tiger that people with desktop Macs will never see. This lesson looks at some simple things you can do to keep from needlessly draining your battery. That way, you don't wind up on an airplane, finishing the last chapter of your book, when suddenly the battery runs out, and….

STEP ONE (Putting Your PowerBook/iBook to Sleep):

If you shut down your computer, it completely turns off, and when you want to use it again, you'll need to start it up from scratch (which takes a minute or two). However, if you're just stepping away from your computer for a few minutes (or even an hour or so), rather than turning the computer off, you can just put it to "sleep." An advantage of putting it to sleep (rather than shutting down) is that it "wakes up" almost instantly, so you can immediately get back to whatever it was you were doing before it went to sleep. This means that when it wakes, all of the documents and applications you had open are still in place from when you last left it (versus when you shut down, which closes all applications and open documents). The Sleep option also saves battery power, because if you stop using your computer for a few minutes, it automatically goes to sleep. You can put your PowerBook/iBook to sleep in one of four ways:

(1) Just close the lid and it will immediately go to sleep.

(2) Choose Sleep from the Apple menu.

(3) You can configure your PowerBook/iBook so it goes to sleep on its own after a period of inactivity that you choose (you'll learn how in the next step).

(4) Press your PowerBook's/iBook's Power On button and a dialog will appear with a Sleep button. Click on that button to put your Mac to sleep.

To wake from the Sleep mode, open the lid or (if it's already open) press any key or click using the scrolling touchpad (or if you have one, use your two-finger scrolling touchpad).

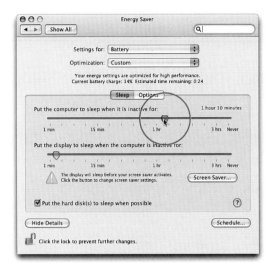

STEP TWO (Setting It Up to Sleep Automatically):

Apple has set up your PowerBook/iBook to automatically go to sleep if there's no activity for 15 minutes. This means if you haven't moved/clicked the mouse, pressed a key on the keyboard, etc. in the past 15 minutes, your computer figures you must be doing something else, so to save battery power, it goes to sleep. Apple chooses 15 minutes, but you can adjust that amount (you can even set it so it doesn't go to sleep at all, which is helpful if you're doing slide show presentations or watching a DVD movie). You do this by first going under the Apple menu and choosing System Preferences. When the System Preferences dialog appears, click on the Energy Saver icon (it's in the center). When the Energy Saver options appear, the Sleep preferences are displayed. At the top of the window, there's a pop-up menu called "Settings For." Click on the menu and choose Battery. Below that, where it says "Put the computer to sleep when it is inactive for," there's a slider (and it's likely set to 15 minutes). For a longer duration, drag the slider to the right. If you don't want it to sleep at all, drag it all the way to the right (to Never). Now click on the small red button in the top-left corner of the window to close System Preferences.

WHEN YOUR COMPUTER IS PLUGGED INTO AN OUTLET

TIP ▶ If you want to choose different settings for when your PowerBook/iBook is plugged into a power outlet (and not running on battery power), go to the Settings For pop-up menu at the top of the Energy Saver window and choose Power Adapter. Now you can drag the slider to select a separate time for that power option (since you're not running down your battery, you can select a longer duration).

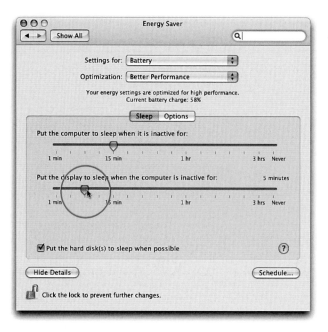

STEP THREE (Saving Battery Power by Putting Your Display to Sleep):
It's helpful to know multiple ways to lengthen the life of your battery
(especially if you're using your PowerBook/iBook on a flight). First, you need
to determine which activities drain your battery the most. One of the worst
offenders of battery drain is the display (also known as your monitor). Hey, it
takes a lot of juice to run that big bright display, so it only makes sense that if
you're not using your computer for a few minutes, you'll want that display to
turn itself off, even before your computer goes to sleep. You can set the time
for your display to "go to sleep" in the same place where you set your entire
computer to go to sleep—under System Preferences, in the Energy Saver
section. If you look under the "Put this computer to sleep…" slider, you'll see
another slider that says, "Put the display to sleep when the computer is inactive
for." Drag this slider to adjust the duration that your display is active. Choose
a length that is less than the sleep time for your system; you want the display to
sleep *before* the computer does to preserve the battery charge. For example, if
you have the computer set to sleep at 15 minutes, you might want the display to
sleep after only 5 minutes of inactivity. Don't worry—the display wakes up even
faster than when the computer itself is asleep, so having the display sleep is even
less of bother. To get the display to spring back to life, just press a key or move/
click with the scrolling touchpad. *Note:* Because the screen saver can conflict
with your display going to sleep, you might want to turn it off. Just click on the
Desktop & Screen Saver icon in the System Preferences window, and when the
Screen Saver options appear, drag the slider to the right (toward Never).

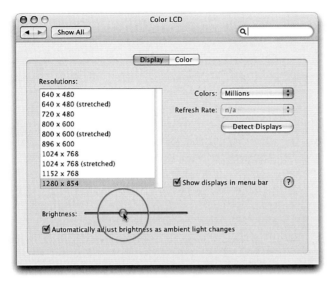

Adjusting brightness through System Preferences

Adjusting brightness using the Function keys

STEP FOUR (Saving Battery Power by Dimming the Screen):
Now that you know the display is a big battery hog, here's something else you should be aware of: The brighter it is, the more battery juice it uses. If you're working on something that doesn't require a very bright screen (for example, you're working on a spreadsheet, a text document, or listening to music), you can dim your screen so your battery will last longer. You can dim the screen in two ways: Go under the Apple menu and choose System Preferences. In the System Preferences dialog, click on the Displays icon. When the Displays options appear, start dragging the Brightness slider at the bottom of the window to the left until your screen gets darker (but not so dark that you can't see). Then, close System Preferences by clicking on the small red button in the top-left corner of the window. Now that was easy enough. For an even faster way, just press the F1 key on your keyboard a couple of times and a large Brightness indicator will appear near the bottom third of your display (the icon kind of looks like the sun). Each time you press the F1 key on your keyboard, your display gets dimmer. Set it as low as you can (while still being able to see what you're working on, of course) to get the maximum battery savings. To increase the brightness again, press (you guessed it) the F2 key.

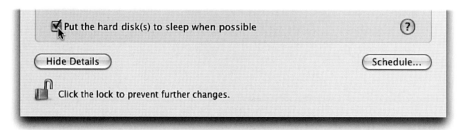

STEP FIVE (Another Battery-Saving Strategy):

There's another little thing you can do make your battery last longer. In the Energy Saver options under the System Preference (where you set the time for when your PowerBook/iBook goes to sleep), there's a checkbox you should turn on. It's named "Put the hard disk(s) to sleep when possible." Ensure this is selected for another way of saving battery life so you can work without power interruptions.

STEP SIX (Shutting Down):

If you want to shut down (turning your Mac completely off), you have two options:

(1) Go under the Apple menu and choose Shut Down. A dialog will appear asking, "Are you sure you want to shut down your computer now?" You can click the blue Shut Down button to shut down immediately or you can just relax, sit tight, and in a few minutes your Mac will automatically shut down.

(2) Press the Power On button once. This brings up a dialog that asks, "Are you sure you want to shut down your computer now?" Click the blue Shut Down button and your Mac will close any open applications and documents, and shut down.

Don't worry if you choose one of these accidentally (or if you just change your mind) because there's a Cancel button you can click to terminate your shut down.

Index